PREACHING AT THE PARISH COMMUNION

4

THE GOSPELS—Series 3, Cycle 1

Hugh Fearn

D1392850

MOWBRAYS
LONDON & OXFORD

Printed in Great Britain by
Alden & Mowbray Ltd
at the Alden Press, Oxford

ISBN 0 264 64590 1

First published in 1972
by A. R. Mowbray & Co Ltd,
The Alden Press, Osney Mead,
Oxford, OX2 OEG

FOREWORD

THE title of this book is *Preaching at the Parish Communion*. So preaching and the sacraments are brought into relationship with each other. This is right. The administration of the sacraments is not the only place where preaching should occur, nor for that matter are other services of worship, nor even the church building, nor monologues, nor spoken words at all; but unless preaching is given an essential association with the sacraments, in due time it will cease to be preaching as the New Testament understands it. All of which does not mean that there ought to be no celebration of the Eucharist without a sermon. What it does mean is that the ministry of the Word and the ministry of the sacraments cannot be torn apart. No wholesome Church can place its emphasis on either Word or sacrament to the virtual exclusion of the other, and remain wholesome.

One of the most devastating criticisms of a preaching ministry could be that it is out of alignment with the sacraments. Take the case of the Holy Communion. What is its irreducible minimum? Surely the breaking of bread and the outpouring of wine, symbolizing the sacrifice of Christ 'for us men, and for our salvation'. There cannot be a celebration of the Holy Communion without these ritual acts, they constitute its essence. And Holy Baptism looks back to the baptism of Christ in blood for all men. It is not for nothing that the candidate is signed with the sign of the cross. The frightening prospect, however, is that a whole preaching ministry, I do not say one single sermon or half a dozen sermons, but a pulpit ministry can continue without being recognizably shot through with the proclamation of the sacrifice of Christ, his death and resurrection. The content of preaching, therefore, must take its cue from the content of the sacraments, and if it does not, it ceases to be New Testament proclamation.

In general terms it could be said that preaching and the sacraments both proclaim the same message. 'For every time you eat this bread and drink the cup, you proclaim the death of the Lord, until he comes' (1 Cor. 11.26). The preaching makes its proclamation in words, the sacraments make their proclamation in actions. This is true. We must, however, be on our guard not to *restrict* the words to the preaching, and the action to the sacraments. There is no sharp dichotomy here. The preaching is not *mere* words. The sacraments are not mere actions. Take the case of the sacraments first. Their administration does not consist of wordless actions. There are words to be spoken at the Eucharist, even correct words, words derived from the sacred tradition, and they cannot be omitted. Consider also the words in preaching. They are not *mere* words. Words rarely are *mere* words. Words are effective instruments. It is true they can bore. But they can at least do that to a whole congregation and drive them away. Words are certainly effective. But at the other end of the scale they can be creative of life. And that is how the Bible understands words. 'By the *word* of the Lord were the heavens made' (Ps. 33.2). And the witnesses of Jesus' preaching asked: 'What is there in this man's words? He gives orders to the unclean spirits with authority and power, and out they go' (Luke 4.36). Preaching then is to be understood as a means of *effective action*. In short, words operate.

This matter of effective preaching needs to be viewed from another angle. Of course a preacher ought to be shown how to do it. He requires guidance in technique. And this he learns more readily from examples than from precepts. It is in fact not the least of the benefits to be gained from reading this book. To teach a preacher how to perform, however, is not all that is required. Indeed, if this were all he were given, it would be better not to teach him at all. Who would be satisfied to instruct the celebrant at the Eucharist just where to stand, where to kneel and what to do with his hands? He must know as much as he can of the meaning of the sacrament. He must know *what* he is doing and why. This involves him in a theology of the sacraments. So too, there is a theology of preaching to be grasped. Not that the preacher preaches it, but he preaches in the light of it.

iv

What is the theology of preaching? It takes its essence from Jesus who 'came into Galilee proclaiming the Gospel of God: "The time has come; the Kingdom of God is upon you; repent, and believe the Gospel"' (Mark 1.14, 15). Jesus' ministry began with preaching, and the content of his message was the presence of the kingdom of God. He did not assert that the kingdom of God was a possible outcome of his preaching, but that the kingdom of God was *already present*, to which fact his preaching drew attention. So Jesus' ministry was in essence testimony to God's real presence with sovereign power in the contemporary. (The 'kingdom of God' means God's kingly rule.) This should be the message of all Christian preaching, not least, indeed mostly, because of Easter Day, Christ *is* risen. There is, however, more to it. Jesus' testimony to God's real presence was not only by means of words, it was also by means of actions. His miracles were in fact disclosure points of God's sovereign action in the present, operative for man's welfare. So Jesus ministered God's sovereign power by words and by deeds, the pattern which underlies the Church's structured ministry of word and sacraments.

One more theological question needs to be asked. Is the Holy Communion only a sign of God's action in the world or is it in itself effective action? The Church of England holds the latter view. Similarly, is preaching only witness to God's action in the world, or is it itself part of the saving action? To go further, when a preacher proclaims Christ, is he only speaking *about* Christ or is Christ also speaking through him? If the latter, then we need not be surprised if the preacher's words are not *mere* words but effective instruments, intruments of healing, instruments of deliverance. As in the ministry of Jesus, words and deeds overlapped to men's temporal and eternal profit, so also in the ministry of Christ now in word and sacrament.

These considerations raise preaching to a high level. There is nothing quite like it in human speech. It stands in a class by itself because of its origin and because of its subject matter. It is certainly not to be classified as sacred rhetoric. Its essence is theological. We must also bear in mind, however, that our theology holds to a theology of the Incarnation. 'The Word became flesh and dwelt among us.' We cannot omit the necessity to earth our preaching. Christian preaching must be *grounded* preaching. This applies to content. There must be homely illustrations, metaphors, analogies and similes. It also applies to form and delivery. The techniques of speaking must be observed. It is at this grounded level that such books as the present publication will help the preacher and through him the congregation. And the purpose throughout is that the preaching, like the sacraments shall be an effective instrument by which the grace of God lays hold of men, and men lay hold of the grace of God.

D. W. Cleverley Ford

In Memoriam
Reginald Richard Roseveare, SSM
my Father-in-God
as Parish Priest in Sheffield
and Bishop in Accra to whom I
owe so much.

ACKNOWLEDGMENTS

The thanks of the Author and Publishers are due to the following for permission to quote extracts: Oxford and Cambridge University Presses, *New English Bible*, Second Edition 1970; Darton, Longman & Todd Ltd, *Jerusalem Bible*.

CONTENTS

x

*The readings for the five Sundays before Advent Sunday are always to be those provided for Trinity 23 and the four weeks following. Readings for Trinity 18 to Trinity 22 will be used according as they are needed.

INTRODUCTION

PREACHING at the Parish Communion is perhaps the most difficult assignment that any preacher can be given. With the promulgation of the new Canons it is now possible for lay men and women in the Church of England to share in that preaching ministry as Readers. It is hoped that this book of sermon outlines will be particularly useful to them as they prepare to preach at the Parish Communion. The occasion of its publication is the introduction of the new Table of Eucharistic Lessons appended to Holy Communion Series Three. This will, it is expected, be authorized for use from Advent 1972, and a rubric states that the readings may also be used at Morning and Evening Prayer on their appointed days. These outlines may therefore be used on occasions other than a Parish Communion, and it is hoped that parish priests seeking a new scheme for presentation of the Faith may find them helpful in their own sermon preparation.

Whether cleric or lay, the preacher at the Parish Communion has a difficult assignment. In the first place it must be charitably assumed that congregations are to some extent committed Christians. Preaching to the converted presents the preacher with the problem of gaining and keeping attention, where there is a familiarity with the gospel passages. It is hoped that the variety of approach in these sermons will give an indication of the variety of preaching which every preacher should seek to develop. This is the only way to secure and maintain interest. Secondly, the time factor requires a clear presentation. This requires as a basis a skeleton structure. Thirdly, we can expect a wide age range and experience range in our congregations at Parish Communion. We cannot satisfy them all in any one sermon and should never attempt to do so. The outlines in this book suggest approaches to meet differing age and experience needs. Fourthly, there is a definite need to relate the preaching to the lectionary readings and in this volume they are related to the relevant gospel passages for Year 1.

The writer of any sermon owes an indebtedness to many

sources of inspiration, not least that of the Holy Spirit. But it is impossible to acknowledge the many writers, teachers and preachers who have helped mould a particular preacher. I would, however, wish to acknowledge my indebtedness to Prebendary D. W. Cleverley Ford, for what I have learned from his books and in sharing with him in the work of the College of Preachers. Few of these sermons have been preached, as the new lectionary was not authorized for use when they had to be prepared for publication. I am therefore particularly indebted to Canon William Purcell of Worcester Cathedral for his comments on my original drafts, but I must accept full responsibility for them all as they now appear. My hope is that they will assist all who exercise a preaching ministry and that in their hands the dry bones of these skeleton outlines will be made to live.

The title of each sermon gives an indication of its theme. For those who wish to announce a text I have given an appropriate one. There is no debate concerning the need to proclaim the *kerygma* in every sermon, applying it to contemporary Christian living, but there is debate concerning the necessity to quote a text at the beginning. On the whole I am inclined to discourage this practice. This is a personal preference and habit; all too often I have heard sermons which have little or nothing to do with the announced text.

My thanks to Mrs. Rosemary Edwards who typed the manuscript for publication and to my publishers, Messrs. A. R. Mowbray & Co. Ltd. I am grateful to The Reverend Wilfred Beale for assistance with proof-reading.

Hugh Fearn

Northwood,
St Philip & St James, 1972

FOURTH SUNDAY BEFORE CHRISTMAS

Observing the signs

St. Luke 21.27 (NEB) *'And then they will see the Son of Man coming on a cloud with great power and glory.'*

INTRODUCTION

Do you drive a car? If so there is little doubt that you will be critical of other road users. Critical of pedestrians who suddenly step off the kerb and ignoring the traffic, cross the road. You will be critical of other drivers, perhaps wondering as they break the Highway Code if they ever passed the driving test. Are we equally aware of our lack of observance of the rules of the road? There are two essential qualities required of the road user: observing the signs and being alert. These same qualities apply to our Christian profession.

The signs ignored

It is extremely important that we should know and observe the signs of the Coming of Our Lord, or we might find ourselves in a situation identical with the people of Israel who did not recognize the Messiah when he came. They mis-read the signs. Signs which were constant in the prophetic inheritance. They asked Jesus for a sign, but none was given except one which they did not recognize. The sign of significance—the cross of Calvary—was not the sign that they anticipated. They looked for deliverance, but their messianic hopes had become political in aspiration. They had forgotten that the Messiah should suffer; that he should be a suffering servant.

The wrong signs

What are the important signs today? Already there are the usual signs of Christmas preparations. Christmas stores are being piled up in our deep-freezes and larders; presents are hid from those for whom they are intended. For many people the signs of Christmas are festivity and frivolity. Tinsel and glitter are held in greater regard than the Babe of Bethlehem whose First Coming we celebrate at Christmastide.

Being alert

As Christians we may also fail to observe the important signs and not be alert to Christ's coming. Genuinely we may seek to understand the mystery of the incarnation. Devoutly we may prepare to receive our Christmas communion. Charitably we may seek to help those in need at Christmastide. And yet we may fail to observe the stirring advent call—'*And then they will see the Son of Man coming on a cloud with great power and glory.*' There is to be a second coming and there will be signs.

Application

We are the Christian observer corps. We are to recognize the signs and to be alert. The signs of tumult and battle are the signs of the enemy in resistance to the presence of Christ. Resistance which at the last will be shaken. There is the sign of expectancy, which requires that day by day we eagerly look for his Coming. There is the sign of liberation and we are to be joyful in anticipation of Christ's coming in power and glory. Knowing the signs we are to be alert.

THIRD SUNDAY BEFORE CHRISTMAS

Search the scriptures

> St. John 5.39 and 40 (RSV) '*You search the scriptures, because you think that in them you have eternal life; and it is they that bear witness to me; yet you refuse to come to me that you may have life.*'

INTRODUCTION

March 16th, 1970. On that day the privileged university

presses produced a best-seller—the *New English Bible* first published in its entirety—Old Testament, Apocrypha and New Testament. A best-seller; the product of years of ecumenical co-operation through which scholars of repute have made available to us an accurate translation in a version more suitable to contemporary understanding. A great achievement; a best-seller; but how is it read? What is our understanding of the scriptures? The Jews searched the Old Testament scriptures for a guide to eternal life. We possess the fuller revelation of the New Testament that eternal life is in Christ Jesus.

Search the scriptures

There may be a bible in every home in this parish. But is it read? How is it read? The scriptures can only be understood by those belonging to the Christian community. The scriptures are the heritage of the worshipping community and enshrined in the liturgy of the Church. Our understanding of scripture springs from faith and the guidance of the Holy Spirit. Tradition and scripture are complementary. Scholars help us to appreciate the deeper significance of the scripture, and to understand societies far different from our own—their customs, cultures and beliefs. Although the bible contains all that is necessary to salvation, it must be interpreted for us.

Testimony

When anyone applies for a new job he produces testimonials or references to give a prospective employer some indication of the kind of person he is; a testimony of character. The scriptures give testimony of who Christ is, and that in him is eternal life. Not in words is our salvation, but in the Word made flesh.

Covenant

Old Covenant. New Covenant. These titles are preferable to the commonly used Old Testament and New Testament. Testament suggests something still to come into effect. '*This is the last will and testament*',—so begins the legal document expressing our wishes for the disposal of property and possessions after our decease. The evidence of scripture is that the new covenant is already operative, through which we share in eternal life.

Application

The bible is the book of the worshipping community. It is not sufficient merely to listen to passages being read in the liturgical worship and expounded in sermons. Each and every Christian should every day read the scriptures, using commentaries or notes to help in a deeper understanding of the old and new covenants. The bible is the Word of God, but salvation is through the Word made flesh; Jesus Christ our incarnate Lord. It is to him that we go for eternal life. Do not be blind like Christ's contemporaries who searched the scriptures believing them to contain the secrets of eternal life and not finding them. Remember that scripture bears witness to Jesus. In him is our eternal life and that is why the bible contains all that is necessary to our salvation. Scriptures record the mighty acts of God more especially in the life, death and resurrection of the Son of God.

SECOND SUNDAY BEFORE CHRISTMAS

Called to action

St. John 1.19 (NEB) *'This is the testimony which John gave when the Jews of Jerusalem sent a deputation of priests and Levites to ask him who he was.'*

INTRODUCTION

In Britain today many question the continued usefulness of traditional institutions. Increasingly individuals and groups question the relevance of 'the establishment' whether in politics or religion. Representative democracy is challenged as not permitting people to be fully articulate and active in politics. It seems to many people that an opportunity to elect members to Westminster once every five years is not sufficient provision for political participation. So we have demonstrations and deputations to Downing Street; and some would urge that there should be referendums on major issues. The Church is similarly challenged and threatened. It is argued (with some truth) that we are too concerned with our ecclesiastical structures (ecumenism, synodical government, liturgical reform) and that the 'institutional' Church does not sufficiently care for the outcasts in society following the example of Jesus in his care for the needy.

When politicians and churchmen are so challenged they react in a manner not dissimilar to the priests and Levites who went as a deputation to John the Baptist in the wilderness. He too was disturbing those in authority by his activities. So they went to enquire who he was. Who are you? What right have you to be active in this way? What is your purpose?

Proclamation

I am not the expected one, nor am I a political agitator. But he is coming, indeed he is here though you do not know him. He is so much greater than I that I am unworthy to unfasten his sandals. The kingdom is at hand.

Response

The appearance of the king demands an immediate response—'*Make straight the King's highway.*' There is no room for the crooked or the narrow. Every one must respond to the Promised One; what will your response be?

Action

This is where John exhibits his activist policy. It was a simple action and symbolic, though profound in its significance and meaning. 'Repent and be baptized.' 'Turn unto the Lord your God.' 'The time is at hand.' There is an urgency about this appeal.

Application

Have we been numbed into a spiritual slumber? Are we really awake to the demands of Christ? 'Sleeper awake!' As Christians we have been baptized into Christ's death and resurrection and have been given a new life in Christ. What is the quality of that life—TODAY? Are we Christian activists responding to the proclamation of John the forerunner? Is there not still the urgency to repent and to actively share in the building of the king's highway. We cannot pray 'Thy kingdom come on earth' and be inactive in seeking to further the kingdom.

THE SUNDAY BEFORE CHRISTMAS

The Lord's servant

St. Luke 1.37 (NEB) ' "Here am I," said Mary, "I am the Lord's servant; as you have spoken, so be it." '

INTRODUCTION

Imagine the situation for Mary and Joseph after the visit of the Angel of the Annunciation, in the stricter conditions of Jewish society. Think of Mary telling Joseph that she was going to have a baby and the circumstances of the conception. There would be much private discussion of the right thing to be done in the circumstances and there is no doubt that Joseph loved Mary very much. He reacted as others would in the circumstances. He planned to send Mary away to a place where she was unknown until the time that the baby was born. But this was not to be. In a dream Joseph was told to act otherwise; and in a few days' time we shall remember that they were travelling together when the time of Mary's delivery drew near. And the babe was born in a stable. Let us prepare for our keeping of Christmas by thinking of Mary and Joseph in their situation; and their response to God.

Responsive to God's will

The angelic greeting to Mary must have been bewildering and

the consequences are unequalled in the world's history. There was the immediate situation: how would people react to her condition; and yet, there was the immediate response from Mary: 'as you have spoken so be it.' Responsive to God's will. Joseph responded to the dream and lovingly provided for Mary and the child; in times of danger to the infant Jesus, all three became refugees in a foreign land.

Responsive servants

Whatever the cost, Mary and Joseph were prepared to be servants of the Lord. Mary responds to the annunciation, 'I am the Lord's servant.' Service for Joseph and Mary was costly. The cost to be measured in the sacrificial cost of Calvary; the shadow of the cross was never far from the crib.

Responsive to God's mercy

Mary and Joseph as the servants of the Lord were conscious of God's mercy. Mary's response in the Magnificat is to praise God for all his mercies; the response of a spirit which rejoices in the Lord. She counts herself blessed as the handmaid of the Lord; chosen by him.

Application

Ever since the coming of Christ there have been men and women in all ages who have responded to God's will, and aware of his loving mercy, have been God's chosen servants. Missionaries in many lands face many dangers and difficulties. Many have willingly embraced the sacrificial demands of the ordained ministry. Yet it is surprising how many Christian parents, committed churchgoers, find it difficult to accept the fact that God is calling their son to the ministry of Christ's Church. All of us are called to ministry in one way or another. How willing are we to embrace that calling? Are we willing to respond to God's will? Being a servant is not an ideal situation; and yet we have the example of Christ before us—'Bearing the human likeness, revealed in human shape, he humbled himself, and in obedience accepted even death—death on a cross.' (Philippians 2.8; NEB).

THE SUNDAY AFTER CHRISTMAS

The greatest gift

> St. Matthew 2.2 (NEB) '*After his birth astrologers from the east arrived in Jerusalem, asking "Where is the child who is born to be king of the Jews?".*'

INTRODUCTION

Mary, Joseph and Jesus received unexpected visitors. Men they did not know. Men who had travelled far. Strangers skilled in astrology, seeking the meaning of a star which had appeared in the night sky. They were Wise Men only in terms of their understanding of their craft or art, which took them first to a royal palace to seek a newborn prince. But they found him elsewhere, and in finding him they were in the presence of the greatest gift that the world has ever known: the person who has most influenced human affairs. For this same Jesus was, and is, 'the way and the truth and the life' (St. John 14.6).

The way

The way in which the Wise Men understood and sought to explain life was by the influence of the stars—they were concerned with the reputed occult influence of the stars upon human affairs. The gold which they brought with them also suggests two attitudes of the way of the world. First, a worldly preference for material wealth and all that money can buy. Secondly, the hopes of many that their future may be foretold by an astrologer and a willingness to pay for such information. There are many today who profess to be able to foretell our future, and many only too anxious to know what the stars foretell. But in the presence of Jesus the visitors realized the inadequacy of their arts. They left behind the trappings of their art—gold, frankincense and myrrh. Here was *the* Way—'no one comes to the Father except by me' (St. John 14.6).

The truth

Many engaged in the practice of astrology would firmly deny

that there is any magic in their art. Indeed many astrologers would claim that they were scientists and that astrology is a reputable science. In earlier centuries the revelation of what the stars foretold resulted in rituals being performed to reverse the fate in store. Frankincense was used in such rituals. But in the presence of Jesus our astrologers realize the futility of such practices and leave behind their frankincense. The truth is that this is God's world and God is the source of all truth, wisdom and understanding. But above all, the truth is that God is Love. In this knowledge we can set aside our fears.

The life

Many fear death. Death has replaced sex as the silent subject of the twentieth century, even in the pulpit. How many sermons are now preached on the four Last Things? And yet for the Christian death has no fear, for life in Christ—'I am the Life' —is eternal life.

Application

There are three important consequences suggested by the visit of the astrologers to Jesus. We must set aside all trivialities of our lives, all superstitions and unworthy actions. We must bring our particular gifts and ask God to use them. But above all we must accept that Jesus is the greatest gift that the world has ever known—he is 'the way, and the truth and the life'.

SECOND SUNDAY AFTER CHRISTMAS

Recognized

St. Luke 2.39 and 40 (NEB) *'When they had done everything prescribed in the law of the Lord, they returned to Galilee to their own town of Nazareth. The child grew big and strong and full of wisdom; and God's favour was upon him.'*

We all like to be recognized. Recognized as individuals and within society. Even the so-called 'drop-out' likes to be recognized as a 'drop-out' and to be accepted as such by other 'drop-outs'. We gain a sense of security by belonging to a family, a group or a nation.

Like other parents Joseph and Mary were desirous that their first-born son should be recognized by name and by society. God also ensured that he was recognized by some as the fulfilment of his promise. Jesus was recognized in the following ways:

By name

Throughout the world there are many traditional naming ceremonies and customs. There are indigenous tribal practices in Africa (in Ghana, for instance), where every child's name includes the day of the week upon which he was born. In England, by law, a child's name must be registered at birth at the local registry office and a Certificate of Birth obtained. There are religious implications in baptism for Christians, as in circumcision for Jews. Jesus, born of Jewish parentage, was circumcised on the eighth day and named Jesus. A name not uncommon in its Hebrew form, *Joshua*, which literally means 'Jehovah saves'. Joseph and Mary gave the Infant Christ the name 'Jesus' by divine command.

By society

When Joseph and Mary brought Jesus to the Temple in Jerusalem they presented him to the Lord. This was in accordance with the Law and provided an opportunity of thanksgiving: two young pigeons, the offering prescribed for parents unable to afford the prescribed two turtle doves. Through circumcision and presentation to the Lord his parents fulfilled the Law and he became a sharer in the Covenant. Thus he was recognized by most of his contemporaries; Jesus the carpenter, Jesus the teacher.

By promise

Some of his contemporaries were to recognize him as the Messiah, the promised Saviour. In the temple were Simeon and Anna. Simeon to whom it had been promised that before he died he should see the Lord's Messiah. Anna, the prophetess who spread the news to all who were looking for the liberation of Jerusalem. Then to the disciples who later proclaimed the crucified, risen and ascended Jesus as Saviour of the World.

Application

In our baptism we receive a name of individual identity and are identified with Christ. We are baptized into his death and resurrection and are partakers of God's promise. We have a recognized security and place within the Christian society. But do we behave in a manner appropriate to children of promise? Do we honour the name of Jesus? Are we recognizable by our words and deeds as Christians—named after Christ? Do we proclaim our allegiance to the Promised Saviour?

THIRD SUNDAY AFTER CHRISTMAS

Sonship proclaimed and tested

> St. Matthew 3.16 and 17; 4.1 (NEB) '*After baptism Jesus came up out of the water at once, and at that moment heaven opened; he saw the Spirit of God descending like a dove to alight upon him; and a voice from heaven was heard saying, "This is my Son, my Beloved, on whom my favour rests". Jesus was then led away by the Spirit into the wilderness, to be tempted by the devil.*'

INTRODUCTION

John did not want to baptize Jesus. He thought it most inappropriate for his baptism was of repentance and Jesus was sinless. Jesus insisted, 'we do well to conform in this way with all that God requires' (St. Matthew 3.15). So Jesus witnessed publicly.

Sonship proclaimed

Immediately after his baptism the relationship of Jesus to God was proclaimed. His sonship was pronounced: 'This is my Son, my Beloved, on whom my favour rests' (St. Matthew 3.17). This unique proclamation has by implication two associated consequences. It makes known the Fatherhood of God, a relationship which Jesus was to encourage his disciples to recognize. It is also the shattering signal to the devil that his time of reckoning has come. Here is the challenger to all that is evil.

Sonship strengthened

The historic ministry of Jesus was about to begin. In the battle which was to lead to the final conflict of Calvary he needed the assurance of the fulness of the Spirit. At his baptism there is demonstrated not only the relationship of Jesus to God the Father, but also to God the Holy Spirit: 'the Spirit of God descending like a dove to alight upon him' (St. Matthew 3.16).

Sonship tested

It is unfortunate that the prescribed gospel passage for today stops short at the end of the third chapter of Matthew's Gospel. In my view it should have concluded with the sentence 'Jesus was then led away by the Spirit into the wilderness, to be tempted by the devil' (St. Matthew 4.1). The proclamation of Sonship had to be proved true. If, as I have suggested, this announcement was also a warning to the devil that the time of reckoning had come, then it was not to be unexpected that the devil would seek to gain an initial advantage. And this he sought to do in the temptations in the wilderness.

Sonship victorious

The New Testament evidence is of the victory of Jesus, the Son of God. He resisted the three temptations in the wilderness.

The devil did not succeed on other occasions. Christ was victor in the Garden of Gethsemane, as well as on the Cross of Calvary.

Application

We are partakers of the victory of Christ. Our baptism proclaims that we are sons of God by adoption. Our sonship will be tested. What really matters is not that we fail; it is that we care whether or not we fail. Then as prodigal sons we determine to return to the Father, and we are overwhelmed by the intimacy of the love of God.

FOURTH SUNDAY AFTER CHRISTMAS

Partnership

> St. Mark. 1.20 (RSV) *'And immediately he called them; and they left their father Zebedee in the boat with the hired servants, and followed him.'*

INTRODUCTION

James and John were in the family business; in partnership with their father, who had taught them the skills of their trade. A trade which was exacting, hazardous and sometimes unrewarding. They were fishermen. Each night at dusk they would sail to the fishing grounds on the lake and, casting their nets overboard, spend the night in fishing. Next morning they would bring in their nets and sail for the shore, but the exacting business was not ended. The fish had to be sorted and marketed by the shore of the lake. The nets had to be put out to dry, and sometimes had to be mended, before they could be used again. An exacting business this partnership with Zebedee their father. It was also hazardous; for sometimes the wind would create a storm on this inland lake and boats had been known to capsize and the crew drown. Sometimes it was unrewarding for they would have toiled all night without any reward; but such was their partnership and business six days every week most of the year round.

But on the seventh day, according to the custom of the people to whom they belonged, no work was done. On this day they went to the synagogue, when they were reminded of the separateness of the Jewish nation; a chosen people, separate from the neighbouring tribes who knew not the Lord God. Occasionally they would go to the temple in Jerusalem and there the separateness of the Holy of Holies was symbolically established by the Veil of the Temple.

Then one day a young teacher came along the shore and said to James and John, 'Follow me, I want you in a new partnership.' At once they left their father and followed Jesus. For three years they went everywhere with their Master. But it was not until after his death on the Cross (when the veil of the temple was rent) that they had to learn what the new Christian partnership meant in the Church. The Acts of the Apostles tells how victory over separatism was won. Now they were in partnership with God in Christ and there was no separation from the brethren, whether Greek or Jew or Gentile.

Application

The use of bread and wine in this eucharist reminds us of the partnership of men with God in the creative activity of the world, satisfying at once our bodily and our spiritual needs. We ought also to be aware that there is no separation between the spiritual worship in which we engage in church and the everyday pursuits of the workaday world. Before we leave this service we shall pray that God will send us out into the world in the power of his Spirit, offering to him our souls and bodies that they may be living sacrifices to him. Here we are in a partnership which is at once exhausting; it involves 365 days in the year. We are in a partnership which is hazardous, for discipleship is costly and some have paid dearly by their very lives. It will often seem unrewarding as we seem to be getting nowhere, but this is illusory if we are filled by a deep desire to serve God.

Our partnership is to be with men, as well as with God. We cannot commit ourselves as a sacrifice to live and work to God's praise and glory and remain satisfied with the situation as it is in the world today. Our good fortune in the bounty of God's gifts, to meet both our bodily and spiritual needs, must make us determined that our Christian partnership stops at nothing to redress the existing possessive and permissive society, which exists in Britain and in the world today.

FIFTH SUNDAY AFTER CHRISTMAS

A sign

St. John 2.5 (NEB) 'Do whatever he tells you.'

INTRODUCTION

It is not always easy to estimate how much food or drink may be required for any particular party. More often than not there is too much refreshment available and some is left over. How much more alarming to discover that there is not enough food or drink for all the guests. Of such an occasion we have heard in today's gospel.

There was a crisis

The occasion was a wedding reception. According to custom wine was drunk by the guests and it would seem that much wine was customarily consumed. Again, according to usual custom, a wine of quality was served at the beginning of the reception and when men's palates were not so sensitive a cheaper wine was used. But on this occasion all the wine had run out. Imagine the consternation of the servants of the household. 'What are we to do? There is no wine.' This anxiety spread and some of the guests became aware of the crisis.

There was faith

When Mary heard of the situation, she found Jesus: 'They have no wine left.' So certain was she that he would help this young couple in their wedding crisis, that even when she received an unsympathetic answer she at once instructed the servants, 'Do whatever he tells you.' The instructions which they received were fantastic; fill the jars with water, draw out with a jug, take to the steward to taste, and then serve the guests. Absurd instructions and yet they fulfilled them. They had faith in Jesus. A fantastic trust based upon what they already knew of his family, his ministry so far and not of his power. For 'This deed at Cana-in-Galilee is the first of the signs by which Jesus revealed his glory and led his disciples to believe in him' (St. John 2.11).

There was a sign

Wine of such quality was brought to the steward to taste, that he criticized the groom for not having served the best wine first. Jesus had changed the water into wine, but before he did so there were three necessary conditions, conditions which are a pattern of many of the other miracles which Jesus performed. Before Jesus performed this miracle there was a need, there was faith and there was co-operation.

Application

At this very eucharist we have the outward sign of bread and wine, which becomes the spiritual food to meet our need. We recognize that need; that is why we are here. We have faith that we shall be nourished by the Body and Blood of Christ. Our co-operation is visibly enacted in the Offertory—the bread and the wine, the products of so much labour of men. Mary said to the servants at the wedding, 'Do whatever he tells you.' In the context of this eucharist let her words remind us as the servants of Christ that Jesus said, 'Do this in remembrance of me.'

SIXTH SUNDAY AFTER CHRISTMAS

The First Team

> St. Mark 2.14 (RSV) '*And as he passed on, he saw Levi the son of Alphaeus sitting at the tax office, and he said to him, "Follow me". And he rose and followed him.*'

INTRODUCTION

The selection of any representative team is made with one end in view: success; and three important standards determine selection: knowledge of the game, the skill and ability of a player in relation to the position for which selected, and team-work.

Jesus had to choose a First Team of disciples, and the gospel today reminds us of the selection that he made of Matthew or Levi. Christ's team was to be representative of himself. He had three years in which to train them to ensure the continuity of his work in the apostolic church. They were a mixed company who responded to his call, 'Follow me.' How do we rate them in respect of knowledge, skills and ability; and team-work?

Knowledge

We would not consider any of the disciples to be intellectuals, nor were they in positions of responsibility in society. Matthew was regarded by his contemporaries as an undesirable associate. Many were simple fishermen. They possessed a wisdom which does not come from books; their occupational experiences made them receptive to the knowledge of God which Jesus wished to impart. He wanted them to *know* God. In the Hebrew language the verb '*to know*' can carry with it a sense of intimate knowledge. 'And the man knew Eve his wife; and she conceived . . .' (Genesis 4.1). The disciples needed to acquire an intimate knowledge of God imparted to them by Jesus in word and deed. 'He who has seen me has seen the Father . . .' (St. John 14.9).

Skills

The ideal relationship with God they saw in Jesus, and there were three particular skills they needed to emulate. First to trust in God that all is finally in his loving care. That was how Jesus trusted. Secondly they needed to follow the example of Jesus in prayer. Thirdly they must have a burning desire to serve. They had the example of Jesus to remind them.

Team-work

This was hard to achieve; they were very human. They were not without ambition seeking preferential positions and the seats of power. How did they become a team? The Holy Spirit at Pentecost enabled them to become a team, but we witness the binding basis of the apostolic team-work in the Upper Room on the night of Christ's betrayal, when Jesus took bread and wine. The Acts of the Apostles records the success of the First Team in the spread of Christianity.

Application

Jesus had chosen his men wisely. The apostles had acquired the necessary skills: trust, prayer and service. We are chosen disciples with a responsibility to work together in Christ's Church. We need to acquire and develop the basic skills of discipleship: trust, prayer and service. We have to learn to work together as a team. The sportsman (whatever his sport) practises daily. As members of the local team we need daily to practise the skills of a Christian and to deepen our knowledge of God.

SEVENTH SUNDAY AFTER CHRISTMAS

Openness to the situation

St. Mark 2.18 (RSV) '*Why do John's disciples and the disciples of the Pharisees fast, but your disciples do not fast?*'

Christians are continually criticized; this should not surprise us. Jesus was criticized for drinking wine; John the Baptist was criticized for his austerity. The disciples of Jesus were criticized for not fasting at a time when the followers of John the Baptist and the disciples of the Pharisees were fasting. The situation when the disciples of Jesus were criticized is linked in the gospel narrative with two sayings of Jesus about behaviour. These two remarks about repairing of clothes and the preserving of wine have a relationship to the answer which Jesus gave to the critics of his disciples' behaviour. These three short statements give a clear guide to Christian behaviour: the characteristic attitude of the Christian is openness to the situation although the Church has not always been faithful to this directive.

Openness to truth

It is much easier to have clear-cut answers, but this is not what the New Testament provides. All too often we defend an already accepted position as doctrinally dependable, when a clear investigation reveals that we have a prejudiced viewpoint. Although it is now a controversy of the past, the attitude of the Church towards Evolution indicates the error of the closed position—that is, when Darwin's original thesis was published —and the benefits of openness to all TRUTH for the deeper understanding of our faith and the liberation of mankind to be truly human. We are not to be afraid of the results of human enquiry or endeavour. There must be an openness to the situation and this requires dialogue rather than dogma; encounter rather than withdrawal.

Openness to love

Whenever the 'area of concern' is large there is the danger of forgetting that we are dealing with persons. This is true of the political sphere. There is a built-in 'danger' in the welfare state. It can become inhuman. The institutional Church is not immune from this danger. Defence of doctrine and adoption of a dogmatic position in defence of truth can itself result in un-loving behaviour. The permanency of marriage which the Church rightly upholds can sometimes result in an unsym-pathetic and unloving attitude to those most in need of loving care—the divorced. This is no easy answer to this situation, but it may well be asked: is the Mothers' Union attitude the right one to adopt? Or again, what should be the Christian teaching about family planning? Was Pope Paul exhibiting an openness to love in his encyclical?

The answer which Christ gave to the critics of his disciples suggests an openness to the situation. You act differently while the bridegroom is with you. Further Jesus emphasized that in all situations we are dealing with persons; persons to be loved, whether unmarried mothers, drug addicts or skin-heads. They need to be loved as they are, so that they may become truly human, for Christ has made us free.

Application

At the time when everything seems to be changing there is a possibility that we wish to see our Church remain firm and resolute. This attitude contradicts the life-blood of our faith for Christ died that he might bring the new resurrection life into being. The bridegroom is no longer with us. He has not left us with clear-cut directions to meet each and every situation, otherwise we could not be free to become ourselves and to help others to realize their human potential. Being truly human requires that we acknowledge that we are made in the image of God. Although we continue to sin, God has always shown an openness to mankind; an openness of truth and love. Are we prepared to be open to each situation in truth and love?

EIGHTH SUNDAY AFTER CHRISTMAS

Challenge

St. Mark 3.2 (NEB) '. . . *and they were watching. . . so that they could bring a charge against him.*'

INTRODUCTION

The newspaper contained reports of two incidents which occurred yesterday. They were not shattering events, yet they indicate a disregard for the sabbath and the traditions of our people. The headlines suggest the contents of the reports:— CORN STOLEN FROM FIELDS; SYNAGOGUE DISTURBANCE ON SABBATH. The two incidents which comprise today's gospel were by no means world-shattering events, nevertheless they were a challenge to the existing powers. Jesus challenged their attitudes towards law, custom and authority.

Challenge to law

The disciples were walking through fields on the sabbath day; they plucked the ears of grain, rubbed them in their hands and ate. They were not criticized for having stolen the grain; they were challenged for having broken one of the many regulations governing the sabbath. Over the years many trivial regulations had been introduced to govern behaviour on the sabbath day. Jesus challenges the critics, 'The Sabbath was made for the sake of man, and not man for the Sabbath.' We can imagine the reactions to this challenge. 'If these regulations are broken and each individual is allowed to behave as he likes where will it all end? Is this the beginning of a permissive society?'

Challenge to custom

The customs promulgated to protect sabbath day observance were many and trivial. They restricted what people could do. There was therefore much speculation in the synagogue that sabbath day when Jesus healed the man with the withered arm. It may well be that this was a contrived situation; the man having been persuaded to be present on that occasion. Jesus knew of this attitude and this grieved him, as his whole approach to life was one of reconciliation and wholeness. Again he challenges: 'Is it permitted to do good or to do evil on the Sabbath, to save life or to kill?'

Challenge to authority

Power can only be exercised if the authority of those in power is accepted. Authority can ill afford to be challenged. In the twentieth century we have witnessed in Africa and South America the overthrow of power in many *coup d'états*. Authority, in order to be secure, must have power and must be respected. Those in authority saw in the action and words of Jesus a challenge to their security and authority in society. Jesus was a danger; a radical, a revolutionary, no respecter of law and customs and authority. The challenge was too dangerous to be ignored. So they discussed together how they might destroy him.

Application

This challenge of authority has a twentieth-century relevance. Christ challenges us today. Particularly does he challenge those who claim to be Christians and are active within the Church fellowship. How far is the institutional Church too concerned with its own structures? Within the organization and administration of the Church are we not all guilty of seeking to maintain entrenched positions? Where does true authority lie? Jesus would remind us that true authority lies with God and the Church is a means to an end and not an end in itself. We are to bring all men into the kingdom of God and this means being concerned with persons as persons, even those who challenge contemporary values: the drop-outs, the hippies and so on.

NINTH SUNDAY BEFORE EASTER

Vision on

St. Matthew 5.8 (NEB) '*How blest are those whose hearts are pure; they shall see God.*'

INTRODUCTION

Television has revolutionized our lives. The impact can be summed up in the words 'VISION ON', which warn that a programme is in transmission; the producer selecting which pictures to transmit to our screens at home. The revolution is that we are all visually conditioned in our thinking. But how do we see God? 'How blest are those whose hearts are pure; they shall see God.'

Seeing God in nature

Many astronauts have orbited around the world in space. Exciting and informative have been the pictures transmitted to earth from the moon's surface. Technological developments have made it possible for twentieth-century man to comprehend more fully the marvels of the universe; a universe so mathematically vast according to the calculations of astronomy. Other scientific calculations indicate the almost incalculable age of the universe, but no scientific enquiry contradicts our religious beliefs. The more we scientifically explore the universe the greater the confirmation of a creative power: God the Creator as expressed in our Christian faith. Then why do not all believe in God the Creator? It is a matter of a true vision. It is as though the universe is a vast television studio presenting the greatest show on earth, but each individual is responsible for selecting the view to be transmitted. The choice is to see God in Nature, but this depends for its clarity of vision upon the individual. The condition is a heart which is pure.

Seeing God in Christ

Many people saw Jesus at work. He amazed his contemporaries

by the authority which he possessed: 'He does all things well. Many people saw Jesus die on the cross, but only a few grasped the significance of what they witnessed; the penitent thief, the centurion at the climax of Good Friday. Only after the resurrection did the disciples really understand the true nature of Christ. 'He who has seen me, has seen the Father', Jesus told Philip. The world still sees in Christ's teaching a way to the brotherhood of man, an ideal ethic for modern man; and his actions encourage activists in contemporary society. But how many see God in Christ? The vision depends upon a pure faith and a heart attuned to God.

Application

A television programme may be well directed, but a good deal depends upon the viewer. Technical faults in one's own receiver may give a distorted picture. Even when the picture which reaches the set is that intended by the director, much depends upon the attitude of the individual viewer. How do you see God? The perfect vision of God remains in the future, but we can see God here and now. The vision has been brought into focus in Christ. We are the receivers of that vision, and the condition for a good reception is that we are numbered among those 'whose hearts are pure'.

EIGHTH SUNDAY BEFORE EASTER

Jesus returned

St. Mark 2.1 (JB) *'When he returned to Capernaum some time later, word went round that he was back.'*

INTRODUCTION

Jesus went away. It was necessary for him to leave town and hide from many people. He had cleansed a man of his leprosy telling him not to tell anyone of the manner of his cure. This request was too much for him to obey. Now he was cleansed it was possible for him to be restored to society and be accepted by the local community. Society needed protection from infectious disease and the priests acted as a primitive preventive medicine agency. To the priests he had to go to receive a clearance and naturally they would enquire of the means of his cure. Jesus went away and hid himself.

Some time later he returned to Capernaum to continue his ministry for God. The news soon spread that he was back in town and the crowd soon gathered at the house where he was staying.

He preached

The house was packed to overflowing as he preached. There was no spectacular display of power to bring them in; no gimmicks. He made known the love of God and the establishment of the kingdom of God. This was Christ the teacher.

They came

The house was crowded where he was preaching. They came to listen to him; some out of curiosity, some to see what he would do and some recognizing that he taught with authority. Others questioned the basis of his authority and his right to act in the way in which he did. Four men brought a paralytic to Jesus; they had not forgotten his healing of the leper and his love of people. They had faith, and so certain were they that Jesus would heal the paralytic that when it proved impossible to gain entrance to the crowded house by means of the front door, they tore away the roofing and let the paralytic down through a hole in the roof.

He responded

Jesus saw their faith: the faith of the carriers who removed every obstacle to obtain access to him; the faith and courage of the paralytic himself in allowing them to lower him into the crowded room. Jesus responded: 'Your sins are forgiven', be reconciled; be whole again. Jesus responded to the critics who accused him of blasphemous conduct and showed his rightful authority, commanding the paralytic: 'I order you; get up, pick up your stretcher, and go off home.'

Application

Sometimes our lives are like empty houses, or so it seems. Our prayers seem unreal and empty and lack all spiritual power. It is as though Jesus has left us and then at that appalling moment of dark despair he returns. Again we hear his voice and our hearts are rekindled with his love. Our faith is strengthened and we hear the comforting words, 'My child, your sins are forgiven.' We are again reconciled and made whole in Christ for God's service.

SEVENTH SUNDAY BEFORE EASTER

Contrasts

> St. John 6.6 (J B) '*He himself knew exactly what he was going to do.*'

INTRODUCTION

Life is full of contrasts. Day follows night; bleak winter gives way to expectant spring; summer splendours are followed by the contrasting beauty of autumn. Scripture is full of contrasts and this is evident in the feeding of the five thousand.

The many

Why did the crowd follow Jesus, ignoring their hunger? They had been impressed by what Jesus had done in healing the sick. They followed him because they were looking for a leader to free them from the dominance of Rome. His action that day in satisfying their hunger only confirmed their impression: 'here is the man to lead us' and they would have seized Jesus and made him king had he not anticipated their plan and made his escape. The crowd believed political action to be the immediate answer to their problems. But Jesus was concerned with the kingdom of God, although in compassion he satisfied their physical needs.

The few

Jesus was aware of their needs. How was their hunger to be satisfied? 'He himself knew exactly what he was going to do', involving 'the Few'—a small boy, a small picnic lunch. He knew that in their apostolic ministry the leaders of the Church would be involved in works of compassion. How would his disciples act? Here was a testing time: 'Where can we buy some bread for these people to eat?' Philip was questioned and gave his assessment of the situation. Andrew was observant and practical: 'There is a small boy here with five barley loaves and two fish, but what is that among so many?' The boy was involved with his small picnic lunch—the few supplies. The twelve were involved in the distribution and gathering up of the food.

The one

Jesus knew the problem. Jesus knew exactly what he would do. He took the picnic lunch; he gave thanks to God; he commanded the crowd to sit down and he satisfied them in the miracle of the loaves, and all were satisfied.

Application

The needs of the world today are manifold. Many seek the solution to these problems in political action. Often the problems are assessed from a standpoint of one's own 'well-being' and shifts in political allegiance can be motivated by dissatisfaction with a goverment in power, rather than a positive belief that an alternative political party can more equitably deal with contemporary needs. Christians cannot remain outside secular society for this is God's world and, in his continuing concern for mankind, God still uses 'The Few'; miraculously using their limited numbers and resources to achieve results out of all proportion to human expectation. We are privileged to be numbered among 'The Few'; how shall we react to God's testing time? We know not what the test will be, nor when it will come. But one thing we know for certain is that God satisfies the needs of all who come to him. Our greatest needs are spiritual and these we must recognize, so that coming to the author and finisher of our faith we may be satisfied.

SIXTH SUNDAY BEFORE EASTER
(Lent 1)

Tempted

> St. Matthew 4.1 (NEB) *'Jesus was then led away by the Spirit into the wilderness, to be tempted by the devil.'*

INTRODUCTION

Jesus had been baptized by John in the River Jordan. His sonship had been declared: 'This is my Son, my beloved, on whom my favour rests.' The proclamation was also a challenge to the devil that here was the challenger to his power in the world. The sonship had been declared and Jesus was led away by the Spirit into the wilderness. A time of preparation for his ministry and a time of testing of his sonship.

Forty days in the wilderness. There was no time like the present so far as the tempter was concerned. Here was a trial of strength, will and power. The challenge was made and accepted. In the temptations the sonship of Jesus was truly tested.

Tell these stones to become bread

Jesus was aware of his relationship to God the Father and empowered by the Spirit he knew his own capabilities. In a position of acute hunger and need, it needed much will-power to ignore the subtle temptation of the devil. Jesus had the power to turn the stones into bread to meet his bodily needs. This miracle could have been performed without anyone else knowing, except God and the tempter. But Jesus refused to use his powers in this way.

Throw yourself down

Jesus had a task to perform: to bring men to understand the nature of the kingdom of God. The tempter suggested an easy way to attract a following. A spectacular leap from the pinnacle of the temple; a glorious display of messianic power. 'This will bring the people running to join you'. But again Jesus stood firm and refused to use such a method to establish his kingdom.

All the kingdoms of the world

Success having so far been denied the tempter, he tries yet a third time. The tempter possesses certain power in the world and he is prepared to offer Jesus the possession of all the kingdoms which he can see from the top of the mountain. There is only one condition: homage to the tempter himself. Not much of a price to pay for privileged power over many people. No! 'You shall do homage to the Lord your God and worship him alone.' Jesus is victorious. This did not mean that the tempter left him alone thereafter. He was tempted time and time again, but he remained sinless.

Application

Jesus was tempted; his followers must not expect to escape from temptation. We shall also be tested. Is that why we pray, 'Lead us not into temptation'? We do not pray that we may have lives without trial. Our prayer is that we shall care whether or not we fail. All of us sin, but the greatest temptation of all is that we should not care whether or not we sin. Jesus cared and that was why he triumphed. We must care. When we fail we must pray for forgiveness. Like the prodigal son we must return to the Father and we shall be amazed by the intensity of God's love.

FIFTH SUNDAY BEFORE EASTER
(Lent 2)

Division is dangerous

St. Luke 11.17 (J B) *'Every kingdom divided against itself is heading for ruin, and a household divided against itself collapses.'*

INTRODUCTION

They were not unanimous in their opinion about Jesus, as they witnessed the cure of a dumb man. Some said he was only able to effect the cure through the powers of the devil; in other times and other places they might even have called him a witch-doctor. Others did not believe that the restoration of a speech defect could be achieved otherwise than by God's aid; but they asked for 'a sign from heaven' to confirm them in their conviction. No sign was to be forthcoming. Instead all were asked to do some thinking about the causes and consequences of 'division' and to arrive at the truth about Jesus in this way.

The divided kingdom

The economic stability of a nation can be irreparably undermined by unofficial strikes and prolonged industrial disputes. In times of war a kingdom is in greater danger of defeat when there are traitors or quislings among the nation. These modern illustrations of national danger arising from a divided kingdom reinforce the truth that Jesus pointed out concerning a kingdom divided against itself.

The divided household

There is some evidence that a child can cope satisfactorily with the premature death of a parent, whereas a child cannot satisfactorily cope with a divorce of parents. Division in the home is not always between parents; there is the division of the generation gap which appears to be somewhat wide in some contemporary family situations. Whatever the causes, or whoever may be involved, division in the household leads to a collapse of relationships in love which are the very foundation of family life.

The divided Church

We are to understand this saying of Jesus—'Every kingdom divided against itself is heading for ruin, and a household divided against itself collapses'—in the context of religious beliefs and action. The basic question had been whether or not Jesus exercised power from God or from the devil. We know Jesus to be the Son of God showing forth the love of the Father. We are part of Christ's Church—sometimes called 'the family of God' or 'a royal nation'. Whether we think of the Church as a family or a nation we have to admit that we are subject to unhappy division—and *division is dangerous*.

Application

'We are the Body of Christ. By one Spirit we were all baptized into one Body. Endeavour to keep the unity of the Spirit in the bond of peace.' We are called upon to reflect at a very personal level on the dangers of division. Ecumenically we are increasingly aware of the dangers of division and there is a welcome move towards unity at the prompting of the Holy Spirit. But how effectively are we dealing with our localized divisions in this congregation? Outsiders are critical of the Church and identify our behaviour as being inconsistent with our professed beliefs. There are many biblical reminders of the ineffectiveness of 'the Body of Christ' where one member is a diseased limb. We must be resolved in our endeavour to maintain unity; a unity which is God-given, a true unity in love. The unity of the Church cannot be manufactured, it is the gift of 'the Spirit in the bond of Peace'.

FOURTH SUNDAY BEFORE EASTER
(Lent 3)

Turning-point

> St. Matthew 16.16 (NEB) *'You are the Messiah, the Son of the Living God.'*

The Boat Race will soon be here. That annual event which attracts so much partisan support on the day itself, although most people have not been to Oxford and Cambridge. At the universities themselves only a minority row and only eighteen men each year represent Oxford and Cambridge. The crews are already on the tideway. Rowing reporters are assessing the performances of both crews and assessments of the outcome of the race will continue until the umpire sets them off on their course. About twenty minutes later radio and television commentators will be analysing the result and doubtless will seize upon some turning-point in the race to explain how it was won or lost.

Life is full of turning-points and the ministry of Jesus is no exception to this general pattern. Today's gospel recalls a significant turning-point which has a continuing effectiveness for the Church today, and a relevance for each individual Christian.

Turning-point for Jesus

Jesus was at Caesarea Philippi, at the foot of Mount Hermon, close to the sources of the Jordan, some 23 miles north of Bethsaida. This was the northernmost place that Jesus reached; a place of seclusion. Here Jesus prepared for the strenuous journey to Calvary, knowing that the ordeal of the passion lay before him. Indeed some commentators regard this event as a crisis-point in the gospel story.

Turning-point for the disciples

Although at the time they did not realize the full implications, this experience marked a turning-point for the disciples. The

profession of faith which Peter made was an apostolic acknow-
ledgment shared by all apostles from that day onward. It was
a turning-point for the disciples in another sense: from that
day onward Jesus began to teach them about the true nature of
his Messiahship, which differed from the popular conception.
It involved suffering and death.

Turning-point for the Church

Only twice does the word 'church' (*ecclesia*) occur in the gospels:
here (St. Matthew 16.18) and in St. Matthew 18.17 (the second
reference refers to the local community and is translated in the
NEB as 'congregation'). We are here concerned with the
universality of the church as expressed in our Lord's words 'And
on this rock I will build my church.' The privileges here assigned to Peter are later assigned to all the apostles (St. Matthew
18.18). Christ is the Church's only foundation (I Corinthians
3.11). 'On this rock' refers to the faith which Peter expressed.
He is the spokesman of this apostolic faith.

Turning-point for faith

The faith which Peter expressed was not of human deduction,
it had been revealed to him by God. This same faith is proclaimed by the Church, and all who hear the gospel have to
answer the same question: 'Who do men say that the Son of
Man is? Who is Christ?' The turning-point is reached when
each individual answers in words similar to those of Peter: 'You
are the Messiah, the Son of the living God.'

THIRD SUNDAY BEFORE EASTER
(Lent 4)

Learning to submit

St. Matthew 17.5 (NEB) *'Listen to him.'*

INTRODUCTION

We listen as much with our eyes as with our ears. Hours

spent before a television screen have this effect upon us. The Transfiguration was a visual presentation of the truth that Jesus Christ is Lord. As we 'listen to him', as God would have us do, we learn that Jesus came not to destroy the law and the prophets, but to fulfil. If he came not to destroy, we must also learn to submit if we acknowledge him as Lord.

Submit to the law

How difficult we find this to do. How do you react to the speed limit when entering a built-up area? It seems so very slow travelling at thirty miles an hour after speeding on the motorways. Any examination of the reasons for the promulgation of such a law reveals that it was passed to protect ourselves against ourselves. The triviality of law enables us to be free.

Are the Ten Commandments of the same nature? The appearance of Moses on the Mount of Transfiguration reminds us that much of the Mosaic law was restrictive: *'Thou shalt not.'* But the very observance of these laws enables man to be free to become his true self. Laws are necessary because of the selfishness of mankind. Jesus gave us two positive commandments: to love God and to love our neighbours. Submitting our wills to the observance of the law—restrictive or positive—enables us to become truly human.

Submit to the prophetic

Elijah and all the prophets were trustees of God's Word; they proclaim, 'Thus saith the Lord.' They proclaim with authority, but their authority is but a pale reflection of the authority of Jesus as we see it in his life and teaching. There was always an urgency about his work and utterance. The triumphal cry on the cross, 'It is accomplished' (St. John 19.30) marks the completion of a divinely imposed trust and task. Throughout his ministry Jesus had been about his Father's business. We need to submit our minds to the authority of Christ; but we shall not find our intellectual capabilities restricted by submission to Christ. We shall find in him a greater intellectual growth.

Moses and Elijah typify all that is best in the Jewish tradition and experience. So overwhelmed were Peter, James and John with their experience on the Mount that they wanted permanently to preserve that experience by the erection of three tabernacles or shelters. This was not allowed; instead they were reminded that God's favour rested upon the Son and they were commanded, 'Listen to him.' When they did listen they were told to keep this vision to themselves; to tell no one. They were also told that Jesus must suffer death.

Application

How are we to listen to him? We listen to Jesus with our eyes as we read the New Testament. We listen to Jesus as preachers proclaim the Gospel. When we respond in faith we learn to submit our wills, our minds and our lives to Jesus the perfector and finisher of our faith.

SECOND SUNDAY BEFORE EASTER
(Lent 5)

Seeing Christ crucified

> St. John 12.21 and 32 (RSV) '*Sir, we wish to see Jesus.*'
> '*I, when I am lifted up from the earth, will draw all men to myself.*'

INTRODUCTION

Jerusalem was crowded as the Passover approached. During the week some Greeks came and approached Philip, 'Sir, we wish to see Jesus.' Who were they? Why did they wish to see Jesus? It could be that these particular Greeks were proselytes to the Jewish faith, but there is no certainty that they were. Inveterate wanderers as the Greeks were, it would be quite natural for them to visit the Temple in Jerusalem. If they were

Gentiles they could at any rate have entered the first of the temple courts. They may have witnessed Jesus overthrowing the tables of the money-changers and those who sold doves. Whatever the reason, they wanted to see Jesus. This should not surprise us. The Greeks were seekers after truth, often trying a succession of philosophies and religions.

Andrew was certain that Jesus would see them, and we can rejoice that this occasion is early evidence that the gospel is for all men. When the Greek visitors asked to see Jesus they would hardly have anticipated that within a few days this same Jesus would be visible upon the Cross of Calvary. Yet the fact and significance of Christ crucified is the pivotal point of our faith. 'I, when I am lifted up from the earth, will draw all men unto myself.'

Application

'Sir, we would see Jesus.' How do we see Jesus? How should we present him to others?

The New Testament Christ

Throughout the ages artists and craftsmen have tried to visualize Christ crucified. The crucifix reminds us of the cost of our redemption, the pains of his passion; the nails through his hands and feet, the body broken, the blood outpoured. The empty cross reminds us that the redemptive act did not end in defeat; his body was taken down from the cross and on the third day he rose again. The Christus Rex (the figure of Christ in priestly robes and kingly crown) reminds us that Christ reigns and reigned from the cross. This is the essential Christ of the New Testament.

Christ in the fellowship

We ought to be able to find Jesus in his fellowship—the Body of Christ. All Christians should be living out the life of Christ in the fellowship of his Church. We fall short of this ideal through our own sinfulness and selfishness, and in this failure we are not presenting Christ to the world as we should. Others ought to be able to see Jesus in us: our lives conformed to his example, strengthened by his Spirit, lived out in his presence.

Christ in the eucharist

The night before his death Christ took bread and wine. He gave us a command, 'Do this in remembrance of me.' By faith and in faith the bread and wine of the eucharist become for us his body; his blood. The service may be one of great ceremonial and majestic music. It may be the simplicity of a celebration in the early hours of the morning or in the quietness of a sick person's room. In all cases Jesus is present. 'Sir, we wish to see Jesus.' There he is in the Most Holy Sacrament of the Altar— his presence felt, although he now reigns victorious in heaven.

THE SUNDAY BEFORE EASTER
(Palm Sunday)

Expectations

St. Matthew 21.10 (NEB) *'When he entered Jerusalem the whole city went wild with excitement.'*

INTRODUCTION

Excitement was mounting, as it always did at that time of the year. There were still a few days to go before the feast, and many people had gathered in the city. There was the opportunity to see relatives and friends. An extra few days made the journey worthwhile, especially if you had travelled some distance. Not infrequently a caravan party would be arranged from the same village, so that the journey could be undertaken in safety and company.

And now they were in Jerusalem in readiness for the Passover feast. The city was crowded; tension mounted as the excitement grew. Already in the temple courtyard the money changers and the stallholders were prepared for this annual invasion, so profitable to them. It was the day after the Sabbath and a small party was approaching the city. On this particular group our interest is centred; we are not unlike the crowd that Palm Sunday.

Expectation

The prevailing political circumstances gave particular significance to that Passover feast. There was a puppet king, Herod; but effective government was in the control of imperial Rome. Roman soldiers paraded the streets. The Jews were permitted to exercise their peculiar religious rites, but Pilate the governor kept a careful watch on the situation. He made elaborate plans for this Passover period, as there might be some disturbance of the peace. And what a disturbance there was on the Friday following.

Many of the visitors hoped for the overthrow of the imperial power. It was like being in slavery once more. In the past had not God delivered them from the power of the Egyptians? In keeping the Passover feast they recalled the mighty deliverance from Pharaoh (who through many plagues had remained obdurate). Moses had been their deliverer then; who would be their deliverer now?

It was well known that the Jewish leadership felt challenged by Jesus. Would he come to the feast? If so, might not this be the occasion for display of leadership? There is no doubt that the crowds would have followed him in an attempt to overthrow the imperial power. This explains their triumphal greetings; and the reversal of their mood on Good Friday, when their expectations had not been fulfilled.

Fulfilment

So high were the crowd's expectations that they did not really notice the contrasting behaviour of our Lord. He did not enter Jerusalem leading a force of fighting men, recruiting zealots as he went along the road. No! He instructed his disciples to bring a colt and he rode into Jerusalem in humility. It was towards evening when he entered the city. But he did not remain there to plan any *coup d'état*. Having visited the temple he returned to Bethany with the Twelve.

Application

As Christians we have many expectations. This is particularly true of our approach to God in prayer. We expect the answer to prayer which we desire, even though we may carefully include a petition that all may be in accord with God's will. When God's will does not accord with ours and the fulfilment is different to the expectation, what do we do? Give up prayer? Question the necessity for prayer? Let us remember the expectation of the crowd on Palm Sunday and the fulfilment. But let us not turn against Jesus, as they did on Good Friday.

EASTER DAY

He is risen

St. Mark 16.6 (RSV) *'He has risen, he is not here.'*

INTRODUCTION

It was the first day of the week and the sabbath day of rest was over. It was early in the morning; the rising sun casting long shadows as three women hurried along the streets. There were shadows in their hearts at the task they expected lovingly to perform.

They came

They were on their way to the tomb with aromatic oils to anoint the body of their friend and Master, who had been hurriedly buried at dusk two evenings before. Sabbath restrictions prevented their coming to the tomb yesterday. Now, at the earliest possible moment, they came; their hearts heavy with sorrow, intending lovingly to perform this last service for Jesus. On their way—Mary of Magdala, Mary the mother of James and Salome—they had been concerned about gaining

41

entrance to the tomb. Did they know that the chief priests and the Pharisees (with Pilate's permission) had put seals on the stone and mounted a guard? Whatever the grounds for their concern—it may only have been the weight of the stone that worried them—they were amazed when they came to the garden.

They saw

They saw that the entrance to the tomb was open. This was the beginning of a totally unexpected experience for the three women as they entered the open sepulchre. They were further astonished to find a young man robed in white seated on the right hand of the tomb. Astounded as they were at his presence, they were amazed at what he had to tell them. They discovered in no uncertain terms that the tomb was empty. 'See, the place where they laid him.'

They heard

It was the rest of the message which proved important, although their hearts pounding at the unexpected encounter meant that they did not immediately realize the import of the good news. 'He has risen, he is not here.' They could see for themselves that the body of the crucified Jesus was missing. Could they really believe that Jesus was going before them to Galilee and that they would see him again? They were alarmed at the content of their commission, to go and tell the news of the Risen Christ to his disciples. And so they ran. Peter and John confirmed the evidence of the empty tomb. The Risen Christ appeared to his disciples. 'He has risen'; Alleluia!

Application

Our experience of the Risen Christ is, in a sense, the reverse of that of the two Marys and Salome. We first *heard* the news of Christ's resurrection. In the biblical evidence and the continuing life of the Church we see that there is, for those who accept in faith, a definite belief that 'on the third day he rose again from the dead'. We come to offer to God our praises and thanksgivings on 'the first day of the week': each Sunday is a

reminder of the mighty act of God in the Resurrection of our
Lord and Saviour Jesus Christ. Alleluia! 'He has risen.' The
liturgical provision for Easter Day is sufficient in itself. There
is little more for us to comprehend than the fact that 'He has
risen'. We need time, after the excitement of the early morning encounter, to appreciate what is the new life in Christ.

THE SUNDAY AFTER EASTER

The Risen Christ speaks to man's condition

> There is no text for this sermon. If time permits it is
> suggested that the gospel passage (St. John 20.19–29)
> be re-read at the conclusion of the sermon.

INTRODUCTION

> 'All the world's a stage,
> And all the men and women merely players;
> They have their exits and their entrances;
> And one man in his time plays many parts.
> His acts being seven ages.'

Shakespeare speaks of the experience of man from infancy
to old age and death. The Risen Christ speaks of the five conditions of man. Herein lies a great difference. The five conditions of being human are not successive stages of experience.
They can apply at any time to each individual, no matter
what is the age of a particular person.

Fear and doubt are frequent experiences in our lives. Fear
may be real or imaginary. Christians are not immune from
this experience. The disciples were behind locked doors for fear
of the Jews. Would they also be regarded as dangerous to the
established religious and civic authorities? These were real fears
in the minds of the disciples in the upper room. They were also
bewildered by reports that Jesus had risen from the dead.
Thomas continued to have doubts until the Risen Christ appeared to him.

It was to this condition of fear and doubt that Christ spoke, showing himself as the crucified one and their Risen Lord. He then spoke to their immediate condition of fear and doubt, 'Peace be with you.' The disciples experienced, as we can experience, the assurance of an inward peace in the midst of danger and uncertainty. The same Risen Christ speaks to us, gives to us that inward peace; a security of mind and spirit even though we are perplexed by the circumstances of our daily lives.

Here was the Risen Christ and the assurance of his voice, 'Peace be with you' rejoiced the hearts of the disciples. 'So when the disciples saw the Lord they were filled with joy.' Christians should be joyful. Let us exhibit joy as the outward expression of our faith.

The disciples were then the recipients of the promised Comforter. 'Receive the Holy Spirit.' This is the condition of man which makes all the difference. Power given by God; promised by Jesus. The certainty of the indwelling Holy Spirit gives us assurance of peace in the midst of the uncertainties of life.

What was the purpose of the gift of the Holy Spirit? The disciples were not to remain permanently in the presence of the Risen Christ. They were to go out into the world and to face the realities of proclaiming their faith in a hostile situation. They must have had many doubts and fears. Doubts when the Second Advent did not quickly come that they had misunderstood the teaching of Jesus. Fears when they were persecuted and faced martyrdom. Yet in all this experience they found the Peace of the Lord and the power of the Holy Spirit.

Application

The disciples had the privilege of seeing the Risen Lord. We are promised the same gifts of peace and power—'Happy are they who never saw me and yet have found faith.' The condition is one of faith. There is a peace to be experienced at each eucharist, and there will be many times when we wish we could remain here in the presence of the Lord. We are not permitted such an escapism. We have to face the fears, doubts and joys of the world through the seven stages from infancy to death.

Always we are assured of the peace of God, the peace of the Risen Christ and the peace of the empowering Holy Spirit.

SECOND SUNDAY AFTER EASTER

On the road

St. Luke 24.35 (NEB) *'Then they gave their account of the events of their journey and told how he had been recognized by them at the breaking of the bread.'*

INTRODUCTION

We can imagine the bewilderment and consternation of the disciples on Easter Day. The women bring the news that the tomb is empty; this is confirmed by Peter and John. There would be concern for their safety as they wondered what action might be taken against them in view of this new development. There was bewilderment as they sought an understanding of the events of that weekend. The day is now far spent and two of the disciples are on their way home to Emmaus, discussing these events; events which have temporarily shattered their hopes. Then Jesus accompanies them, 'but something kept them from seeing who it was.' This story is so well known to us that it may have escaped our notice how Jesus deals with them.

He listens

Jesus enters into conversation with them, and they are surprised at his apparent ignorance of what has happened in Jerusalem over that weekend. They tell him all. That Jesus had been arrested, condemned and put to death. That they had hoped that Jesus would have liberated Israel. And now it was being claimed by some of his followers that 'he is alive'.

He speaks

Although the disciples had shared a life with Jesus during his ministry, they had not clearly understood his mission. Their hopes had been that he would liberate Israel. What kind of liberation? Were they looking for a political liberator who would free Israel from the domination of Rome? The liberation that Christ had brought was a liberation from sin. And so Jesus begins to teach them again concerning the true nature of the Messiah; how that he must suffer; that his glory shone from the cross. He does this by reference to familiar prophetic writings.

He acts

It is in their home that they recognized him. They recognized him by his actions as he blessed the bread, broke it and distributed to them.

They respond

This episode on the road to Emmaus gives us an example of the ideal relationship of a disciple to the Lord. Jesus listens, speaks and acts; they respond. There was a willingness to allow a stranger to join them on their journey and share in their personal conversation. Jesus encouraged them to reveal their fears and their hopes; and they told him all. We can imagine how they listened as Jesus talked, setting their hearts on fire as he explained the scriptures to them. Their response to his revealing of himself was to return to Jerusalem at once. No question of being tired; it will do tomorrow. They were impelled to return to the other disciples and tell what had happened on the road and how Jesus was known to them in the breaking of the bread.

Application

As the disciples of Jesus we can experience the same relationship to our Risen Lord at every eucharist. He makes himself known and available to us in the bread and the wine. But first he listens to us, to the secrets of our inmost hearts for from him 'no secrets are hid'. He listens as we offer our adoration and make our oblation. He speaks to us in the scripture readings, if only we would seek to understand them in the light of his Resurrection. How shall we respond?

THIRD SUNDAY AFTER EASTER

Out of the deep

St. John 21.14 (NEB) '*This makes the third time that Jesus appeared to his disciples after his resurrection from the dead.*'

INTRODUCTION

They had all left their secular employment to join in a new enterprise, with no extensive analysis of the security or prospects offered in the new engagement. They had simply been attracted by the personality and call of Jesus: 'Follow me.' The life they had experienced for three years as disciples had been exciting, enthralling but never secure; and now all that was over. One Passover week in Jerusalem had changed everything. The leader whom they had hoped would liberate Israel had been arrested, tried and put to death. He had since risen; of that they were now certain. They had received instructions to go to Galilee. What were they to do when they arrived there? Several of them had been fishermen. Seven of them decided to enter into parnership, Peter giving the lead. 'I am going out fishing.' 'We will go with you.'

It was night

It was only a few nights previously that they were all together in an upper room preparing for and keeping the Passover; that was the night when one of their number betrayed Jesus. It was night when Judas went out to deal with the enemy; a night which turned their hopes into nothing. Another night; their labours have availed nothing; they have toiled all night and caught nothing.

It was dawn

As they approached the lakeside there was a lone figure on the shore. In the light of the early dawn they did not recognize him. This dawn Jesus speaks again: 'Throw your net overboard on the starboard side.' They did so, and they landed an amazing catch. When God was with them their work was fruitful. They had temporarily turned away from their calling as disciples ('fishers of men'), a temporary apostasy; yet God was with them now in their secular employment. From night to dawn; from nothing to plenty, and the net didn't even break.

There was a charcoal fire

Jesus knew their every need; their physical hunger that morn. He had prepared a charcoal fire, and asked them for some of their catch; before long he was feeding them with bread and fish. This was 'the third time Jesus had appeared to his disciples after his resurrection'. They knew it was the Lord; and as they ate, they may well have recalled the occasion when Jesus had fed the multitude from a small boy's picnic lunch. The Risen Christ was no phantom; he shared their meal. The resurrection was to transform their lives as once again after his Ascension they left their secular employment and became active apostles.

Application

In this episode by the lakeside we can again discern a pattern by which Jesus worked; the same pattern by which God works in relation to us today. He calls: 'Friends have you caught anything?' He commands, 'Shoot the net to starboard, and you will make a catch.' He provides, 'Come and have breakfast.' William Temple in his *Readings in St. John's Gospel*, writes:

> 'So often the message of the Lord reaches us through some experience or acquaintance reckoned at the time as ordinary and commonplace. Only afterwards, and in the light of results, do we realise what or who was really in touch with us through the apparently commonplace event or person. . . . What is done in obedience to the Lord's command,

even though He who gives the command is not recognised, results in overwhelming success. When His disciples have obeyed His command, the Lord himself offers them refreshment and sustenance'.*

FOURTH SUNDAY AFTER EASTER

Peter

St. John 21.19 (part) (NEB) *'Peter was to glorify God. Then he added, "Follow me."'*

INTRODUCTION

Today's gospel is the continuing story (from last week) of the third occasion when Jesus appeared to his disciples after his resurrection. Let me remind you. Going to Galilee seven of the disciples had returned to their secular employment of fishing. They had fished all night and caught nothing. Obeying the command of Jesus from the shore they landed a tremendous catch; they then breakfasted with him. It was Peter who had taken the initiative in returning to their secular employment: 'I am going out fishing.' It was Peter, once Jesus was recognized by the lakeside, who immediately plunged into the water and hurriedly waded for the shore. It was Peter with whom Jesus began conversation after breakfast.

The rock

It was at Caesarea Philippi that Jesus had first indicated that Peter was the 'rock' upon which he would build. Jesus knew Peter well; his failings as well as his virtues. The occasion of this proclamation was the assertion by Peter that Christ was the Son of the Living God.

The rock falls

Rock suggests firmness and we have our Lord's story of the house built upon rock rather than shifting sand. Any geologist knows that rocks differ in composition, and observations

---

*William Temple, *Readings in St. John's Gospel*, Macmillan: St. Martin's Library paperback edition, pp. 380 and 381.

around the sea coast, as at Hunstanton in Norfolk, reveal that rocks crumble and fall. The rock, Peter, fell. In spite of advance warning Peter denied our Lord. In the circumstances of the arrest of Jesus, his fears for his own safety made Peter put himself first and he denied Jesus. And like many of the other disciples on Good Friday he deserted the Saviour.

The rock re-inforced

When there is a danger of disintegration steps can be taken to strengthen foundations. This is precisely what Jesus was now doing for Peter on the shores of the lakeside. Peter's confidence had been shaken, so that he could depend upon that firmer rock, Christ himself. The three-fold questioning of the loyalty of Peter corresponds to the three denials. The answer was almost always the same: 'Then feed my lambs'; 'Then tend my sheep'; 'Feed my sheep.' Peter was restored to his discipleship, that he might glorify God.

Application

The initiative still rests with God. We must respond and in the Series Two Confirmation service the affirmation of faith made by the candidate is very definite: 'I turn to Christ.' Like Peter we may fail; it is almost certain that we shall. If Jesus can take a fisherman like impetuous Peter and bring him to that witness which we find in the Acts of the Apostles, he can take us. By the grace and mercy of God we can become more perfect. In each eucharist that grace and mercy is re-inforced. Each one of us should be a rock upon which Christ can build; but the true rock is Christ.

FIFTH SUNDAY AFTER EASTER

Plain speaking

St. John 16.25 (NEB) '*Till now I have been using figures of speech; a time is coming when I shall no longer use figures, but tell you of the Father in plain words.*'

Generations of Christian preachers have exercised ingenuity in interpreting the parables of Jesus. The many differing aspects of a particular parable have been given a relevant meaning. Recently emphasis has been on one relevant meaning for each parable. Whether or not ingenuity in interpretation or single-mindedness in interpretation is the right way, it remains true that each parable has a relevance for understanding God's purposes and the nature of his kingdom. Jesus spoke to his disciples, as well as to the multitude, in figures of speech. Now he begins to speak plainly to them and to us.

The word *parœmia* is the word used for Jesus' parables and we can perhaps best translate this as 'a saying that is hard to understand'. A parable needs deep thought before it can be appreciated and our understanding of it is dependent upon our acceptance of the eternal truths which Jesus taught. Listen to him as he speaks more directly of these eternal truths.

He speaks plainly—I come from God

Jesus is making a stupendous claim which expresses his relationship to the Father. All that is embodied in the Incarnation is contained within this claim: 'I came from the Father and have come into the world' (St. John 16.28). In other words: 'I am the Son of God—before Abraham was, I am—In the beginning was the Word, and the Word was with God—the only begotten of the Father, full of grace and truth.'

He speaks plainly—I go to the Father

'Now I am leaving the world again and going to the Father' (St. John 16.28). The disciples recognize this as plain speaking. But Jesus still has to explain the way of his return—the Way of the Cross. His work in showing forth the love of the Father is not yet complete. The death upon the cross has to be endured. His disciples are to see this as a victory: 'I have conquered the world.' The truth was proclaimed in the triumphal cry from the cross: 'It is accomplished.' The victory was on Calvary; it was made known the third day.

He speaks plainly—approach God direct

God loves us. The death on the cross was not to appease God. All too often men have contrasted God in anger with gentle Jesus. The promise that we can approach God was made *before the Passion.* Jesus came because God so loved the world. Ours is the God of Love. The way for every man is open to God.

He speaks plainly—have courage

The disciples' allegiance would soon be sorely tested. Jesus, in whom they had placed their trust, would be tried and ignominiously put to death. They would almost wish that the ground would open up and swallow them. So Jesus must warn them of the trials which lay ahead; immediately and in their future apostolic work. Their lives will be shattered. They will be scattered abroad. Courage! 'I have conquered the world.'

Application

We have access to the Father through the Son. Our prayers are concluded in his name. We have access to the Father, our God of Love. As followers of Christ we must expect to encounter difficulties in our discipleship. Above all we need courage to endure. Victory is certain, though we too must travel the way of the Cross. 'Take up thy Cross', the Saviour said. This is plain speaking. It demands an undeviating response.

SIXTH SUNDAY AFTER EASTER

Last instructions

> St. Luke 24.48 (NEB) '. . . *it is you who are witnesses to it all.*'

INTRODUCTION

Once more the unexpected has happened. Headlines typical of the occasion have been placarded across our newspapers: 'The Giant-Killers.' A hitherto unknown non-league club has beaten a First Division team in the Fifth Round of the Cup. It is this possibility which makes the F.A. Cup competition so attractive for many soccer fans. The unexpected has happened again; but it was not an unplanned victory. As soon as the manager knew the team against which they were drawn, he went to see their opponents play. He assessed their strengths and weaknesses. Tactically he began to plan for success; bringing his team into his confidence, as he outlined his scheme for victory. The day arrived; just before the match began, and at half-time, he gave them their last instructions. Then it was up to the team. His planning and training paid dividends. The unexpected happened.

When we consider the beginnings of the Christian Church with the twenty centuries of its history, we might well be excused in thinking that 'the unexpected has happened'. Not unexpected, in the planning vision of Christ. Not unexpected once the disciples had received the gift of the Holy Spirit at Pentecost, when they became transformed men. The task which confronted them demanded that they be giant-killers. And so they received their last instructions from Jesus.

God's plan complete

Jesus began his last instructions by referring to God's plan as revealed in the law and the prophets. This plan has now been completed. This they understood as Jesus revealed the meaning of the scriptures. Then he reminded them that in the upper room he had explained to them that the Messiah must suffer and die. He had demonstrated to them in his resurrection appearances that victory had been gained in accord with God's Plan.

The effectiveness of God's plan

The victory of Christ on the cross was not to be headline news for one day only. The effectiveness of that victory was to be continually proclaimed; the forgiveness of sins. The conditions of sharing in that victory were: proclamation of the fact of man's redemption *and* repentance in response to that proclamation.

The implementation of the victory

Victory has been won. Man's salvation is assured. The spread of the gospel depended upon two conditions: knowledge and power. Knowledge the disciples possessed from their experience of being with Jesus. They were witnesses; their knowledge and understanding of what they had witnessed was then deepened and enriched by the Holy Spirit. The power to proclaim was given by the Holy Spirit. Over the centuries the Holy Spirit has guided generation after generation of Christians in a deeper understanding of the divine plan.

Application

The partisan supporters cheerfully proclaiming the victory of their team are witnesses to an event which they have seen. A witness is called upon to state (if necessary under cross-examination) the occurrence as he has seen it. We are called upon to witness to an event we have seen through the proclamation of others and through the indwelling power of the Holy Spirit. We are aware of the last instructions of the Risen Lord before his ascension, and are able to assess the validity of these instructions against the background of the victory of Christ.

PENTECOST

Switched on

St. John 14.15-17 (JB)
'If you love me you will keep my commandments.
I shall ask the Father,
and he will give you another Advocate
to be with you for ever,
that Spirit of truth
whom the world can never receive
since it neither sees nor knows him;
but you know him,
because he is with you, he is in you.'

If you want to convince someone of the divinity of Jesus and to underline the firm belief and trust of Christians in the person of Christ, ask them to read the final discourses of our Lord with his disciples, in the thirteenth to seventeenth chapters of St. John's gospel. Ask them to consider the content of that teaching and prayer against the background that Jesus knew that the next day he would be put to death upon a cross. Note his concern for his disciples: 'I will not leave you orphans.' He was concerned that they should accept their role as founder-apostles of his Church. All this against the urgency of the morrow— the cross on Calvary. In today's gospel we have one short extract from what Jesus said and did that night in the upper room, and this concerns the gift of the Holy Spirit. The gift of the Father; promised by the Son.

Love and obey

Love is essentially related to persons. True love evokes obedience and that is why it is not inappropriate for a bride at her wedding to promise 'to obey'. This is not a relic of a society dominated by males; it reflects the dual responsibility and love for each other. No husband, who truly loves his wife, would expect obedience to any wish or command which was inconsistent with that love. The marriage service further proclaims that the ideal relationship between a man and his wife is 'the mystical union that is betwixt Christ and his Church'. Taking this truth in reverse application, it can be demonstrated that the ideal marriage indicates that intimate relationship in love which Christians ought to have with Christ. Our response is loving obedience to his commands, and on his part there is the promised gift of the indwelling Holy Spirit.

Advocate and leader

The continuing provision of an advocate for us is a further indication of God's love for us. God cannot act contrary to his own nature; he must therefore judge righteously. Of his love (promised by Jesus) he has provided us with an advocate, the Holy Spirit. Our response to God's love depends upon knowing him and his purposes. We must know him—and that is why the Holy Spirit is our leader; he will lead us into all truth. The world (as distinct from Christians who have received the gift of the Holy Spirit) do not know him because they are bemused by the cleverness of man. They speak of scientific truth as the criterion by which all truth is to be judged; truth demonstrable in the laboratory. The world is bemused by the cleverness of linguistic philosophers. Yet the only pre-requisite to knowledge is a simple faith. The Holy Spirit will guide us into all truth. For truth is of God.

Application

What is our knowledge and experience of the power of the Holy Spirit? The Holy Spirit is power; a gift received from God in baptism. 'He is within you', Jesus promised. But power has to be effectively used; a TV set will not provide any sound or vision unless it is switched on. The Holy Spirit is power within us; a power which transformed the disciples on the feast of Pentecost. We have that same power—are we switched on?

THE SUNDAY AFTER PENTECOST

A life full of promise

> St. John 14.12 and 13 (NEB) '. . . *he who has faith in me will do what I am doing; and he will do greater things still because I am going to the Father. Indeed anything you ask in my name I will do, so that the Father may be glorified in the Son.*'

INTRODUCTION

A young mother proudly pushes her first baby in his pram. Dependent upon the mother's care, here lies a life full of promise. I wonder if that life full of promise will be fulfilled? Next time you see a mother pushing her baby in the pram reflect that your life also is a life full of promise. In your life full of promise you will make many promises; none more important than those made in confirmation.

You will do what I am doing

What was Christ doing? He was showing people what God was like. He did this in preaching and teaching, and his contemporaries were impressed by the authority with which he spoke. Jesus showed what God was like in his compassion— the care of the sick and needy, befriending the outcasts of society—work of reconciliation. Think of his parables. Think of his miracles. This was the work which Jesus was doing, and he promises his apostles and all men and women of faith that we can do these same things.

You will do greater things still

Jesus promised not only that his followers will do as he did; he promises that they will do greater things. Throughout the centuries of Christianity his promise has been fulfilled through the corporate ministry of the Church. On earth Jesus' preaching and teaching was limited to three years active ministry, and to a very small geographical area. Beginning with the apostles the area of proclamation has spread throughout the world. The healing ministry of Jesus was similarly limited in time and space. Now medical resources bring healing and reconciliation to men, women and children in hospitals, infirmaries and dispensaries throughout the world. Fulfilment in lives of promise; for Jesus is still active in his Church. How is this possible?

Ask and I will do

Jesus not only taught and healed; he was constantly praying. Follow his example, and there will be an answer to prayer. Prayer is a power when rightly used. 'Ask in my name'; and we do as we end our prayers with the words, 'through Jesus Christ our Lord.' Asking in the name of Jesus implies that the prayer we offer is prayer which Jesus would offer. This is a useful criterion to apply to our prayers: is this the kind of prayer that Jesus would make?

Application

All share in a life of promise through faith in Christ Jesus. The promises which Jesus made to his apostles are being fulfilled in accord with God's purpose. Is the life of promise which is yours and mine being fulfilled? The baby in the pram is a constant reminder that each person possesses a life of promise. We know also that a life of promise can remain unfulfilled. The eucharist in which we share this morning reminds us of the three conditions of a spiritual life of promise. A life of promise is a shared life, in the presence of God, and within the fellowship of the Church. A life of promise is dependent upon a life of prayer, with moments of withdrawal. A life of promise above all is dependent upon the grace and mercy of God.

SECOND SUNDAY AFTER PENTECOST

The true vine

St. John 15.1 (RSV) '*I am the true vine, and my father is the vinedresser.*'

INTRODUCTION

The disciples experienced a relationship with Jesus in the intimate fellowship of his ministry. Our Lord was more aware of this relationship than they were; for he had carefully nurtured it and seen it grow. It was his concern that the relationship should continue after his death. They must be prepared for the challenging circumstances that were immediately ahead; only a short time was left. The betrayer had already gone out into the dark night intent upon his cause. It was only on later reflection, as the Holy Spirit guided them into all truth, that they realized the implication of all that happened in the Upper Room that night. Jesus had washed their feet; setting an example to his servant Church. Jesus had given them directions for the eucharistic remembrance of him. Then he taught them about their relationship to him and the Father; a relationship which is also ours.

In the gospels we find appropriate selection by Jesus of homely illustrations to disclose divine truths. On this occasion Jesus selects the figure of the vine to indicate the true relationship of the disciples to himself and to God. There is a continuity of teaching on this particular relationship throughout the whole of the fifteenth chapter of St. John, and over the next three Sundays we shall be looking at this same theme, developing the theme as Jesus did in the Upper Room.

Today's short extract (verses 1 to 5) establishes that our relationship to God begins with Jesus: 'I am the true vine.' These five words would convey more to the listening disciples than they would to us, lacking the religious inheritance and national history of the Jewish people. They would instantly be aware of the symbolic significance of the vine for the chosen people of God.

> 'Thou didst bring a vine out of Egypt; thou didst drive out the nations and plant it' (Psalm 80.8).

In poetic terms the psalmist tells of the experience of the chosen people. God had rescued them from the captivity in Egypt and brought them to a promised land. He goes on to disclose the failure of the chosen people; they became a fruitless vine. This is a theme which is recurrent in the prophets.

There had been constant pruning by God; but now the true vine had been planted. It is a new stock; Jesus is the true vine. The figure of the vine, which previously had been used to describe the nature of the relationship between a chosen community and their God, he uses to describe his own relationship to God: 'I am the true vine and my father is the vinedresser.' God will continue to prune. There will be fruitless branches in the Christian community. The relationship is firmly established in Christ Jesus, the true vine.

Application

We are grafted into the true vine in our baptism. The relationship is established. Has the relationship been deepened? Do we respond to God's pruning? God is the vinedresser, but he uses men as his implements. The branch is nourished by the whole Body of Christ. The priestly ministry in the administration of word and sacrament is a chosen instrument of God's purpose. The effectiveness of the relationship is certain on God's side: how do we respond?

THIRD SUNDAY AFTER PENTECOST

The branches

> St. John 15.4 and 5 (RSV) '*Abide in me, and I in you . . . I am the vine, you are the branches.*'

INTRODUCTION

Last Sunday we were reminded that our relationship to God is rooted in Jesus; the true vine planted by the Father. The true vine was a new stock, a replacement of the vine which had ceased to respond to the loving care of the heavenly gardener. Jesus is the vine; his purpose to produce successive generations of Christians living in 'fruitful' service to God. We are the branches of that true vine.

Relationship to Christ

'You will know them by their fruits' (St. Matthew 7.16), said Jesus on a different occasion, to distinguish between true and false prophets. The purpose of each branch is to bear fruit, and the relationship of the Christian to Christ is fundamental. 'You did not choose me, but I chose you' (St. John 15.16). All that we do that is profitable to the Lord stems from him. He is the source of our being. We are to be ever aware of this intimate relationship. He is to abide in us, and we in him. Whenever we cease to have this true relationship with Jesus we become useless branches. Our power, our energy is sapped; there is no nourishment.

Purposeful relationship

The branch is to bear fruit. It does not live for itself. The flowers of the vine are small; the fruit more magnificent. No sooner has the fruit ripened than the vinedresser drastically prunes the healthy branch so that it can bear more fruit in due season. Thus we can see the hand of God at work in the Christian community down the ages. Sometimes by pruning the Church of errors of doctrine and living he restores the Church to its purposeful relationship in Christ. Sometimes by grafting-in new branches he ensures that the Church more fruitfully fulfils his purposes. There are many today who would claim that God is requiring particular branches of the Church to die institutionally so that a newer and more effective Church may come into his service.

Unprofitable branches

The stock of the vine is sure and certain. Jesus is the true vine. He died that we might live in him and he in us. The vine is healthy and is in God's care. The fruitfulness (which is the sole purpose of the vine) is, however, dependent upon the branches. Jesus says that God will certainly destroy the unprofitable branches.

Application

If we are to be true to our Christian calling—'You did not choose me, but I chose you'—there are three essential conditions to ensure being profitable branches. Firstly, we must be ever aware of an intimate relationship in Christ and see that nothing severs that relationship. Secondly, the condition of abiding is love. 'As the Father has loved me, so have I loved you; abide in my love' (St. John 15.9). Thirdly, the consequence of abiding is service. So shall we maintain a fruitful relationship.

FOURTH SUNDAY AFTER PENTECOST

True love

> St. John 15.12 (RSV) *'This is my commandment that you love one another, as I have loved you.'*

INTRODUCTION

Our Lord's command to love one another was given to the disciples in the Upper Room, after the institution of the Lord's Supper. It is a command given to the fellowship to love one another, after the example of Christ's love for mankind.

The love of Christ

The love of Jesus is like a precious jewel with many facets. In Christ's ministry we see a compassionate lover dealing with many people in differing ways as he sees their needs. Consider how he dealt with Peter on three different occasions. At Caesarea Philippi he commends the disciple's faith. Later he warns Peter that, in spite of his expressed love for Jesus, he will in fact deny him. After his Resurrection he restores Peter's confidence, 'Feed my sheep'—thus enabling Peter to become truly himself as an apostle. There is no coercion in true love. We see this evident in all Christ's dealings with men.

In Christ's death on the cross we see true love responsive to other's needs. 'Greater love hath no man than this, that a man lay down his life for his friends' (St. John 15.13). The love of Jesus was responsive to God's love—in the Garden of Gethsemane ('Nevertheless not my will, but thine be done' (St. Luke 22.42)); and on the cross of Calvary ('Father, into thy hands I commit my spirit' (St. Luke 23.46)).

The love of God

Christ's relationship to God is announced at the baptism of Jesus: 'This is my beloved Son, with whom I am well pleased' (St. Matthew 3.17). Jesus expressed the relationship in the very words he used, 'Abba, Father'; and when he wished to describe the love of God for mankind he told of the return of a prodigal son. The love of God evokes a response, a response which Jesus made, 'I have kept my Father's commandments and abide in his love' (St. John 15.10).

Application

Our love is a response to the love of God and finds expression in our response to Christ's command to love one another. This loving response has to find expression within the fellowship. Christ's command was given to the disciples for the continuance of their fellowship. Already there had been debate and dissension on the right to places of importance. Jesus set them an example of service as he washed their feet. The Church—you and I—are called upon to be a caring Church following the example of Jesus. But first there must be 'the love of one another in the fellowship'. The command was given to the first fellowship after supper. The command is given to us. Does this congregation obey the command, 'love one another, as I have loved you'? Christians often fail to obey this command. Sometimes over some person or some action they leave and go and join another congregation; or perhaps leave the Church altogether. In the human family, relationships are not always easy, but if the family is to remain a family love must prevail. If the fellowship is to survive it must be based on true love, fulfilling Christ's command: 'love one another.'

FIFTH SUNDAY AFTER PENTECOST

Right priorities

St. Matthew 19.25 (JB) *'Who can be saved, then?'*

INTRODUCTION

Stephen and Jennifer spent their honeymoon in Majorca. They returned to their own home—at least they called it 'our home'; but they had taken out a very substantial mortgage on it. They had delayed their marriage until they had saved sufficient money for the deposit. Capital invested in housing was a sure safeguard against inflation. It was also a safe investment.

Jennifer was house-proud from the start. There must be fitted carpets throughout. A washing machine, dishwasher and TV set were essentials, not luxuries. Stephen was keen on records and appropriate Hi-fi equipment was a 'must' for him. And so from the start they possessed a lovely home, and relatives and friends admired Stephen and Jennifer in their circumstances. The double garage housed two cars; although one was a firm's car.

Possessions were only made possible at a cost. Mortgage payments had to be paid regularly, and some of the furnishings had been bought on hire purchase. Financial commitments meant that both had to go out to work, and Jennifer had to take precautions not to become pregnant. Property ownership they found involved more and more financial costs, as they had to provide for rates, comprehensive insurance and for redeeming the mortgage in the event of the premature death of Stephen.

To some extent they were the slaves of their possessions. The necessity for both to go out to work meant that domestic chores occupied so much of their leisure time. Saturday morning was spent at the shops buying in supplies for the week. During the weekend both cars had to be washed and polished, and Stephen saved some of the costs of servicing the cars by working on them himself. Whilst Stephen was occupied mechanically beneath the cars, Jennifer went to the launderette to cope with the week's washing. Throughout the year, particularly from spring to autumn, the garden needed constant attention: lawns to be cut, weeding to be done and so on. All this leisure time employment left them with little spare time to enjoy their possessions.

They were law-abiding citizens and would not dream of hurting anyone or any animal. At one time Jennifer had been a keen opponent of blood sports and a supporter of anti-vivisection. Their marriage vows meant everything to them, and there was never any question of another man or woman in their lives. They performed neighbourly acts of kindness. Indeed they would both claim to be living a good life.

Application

But to Stephen and Jennifer Jesus may well say, 'If you wish to be perfect, go and sell what you own, and give the money to the poor, and you will have treasure in heaven; then come, follow me' (St. Matthew 19.21 J B). Why should Jesus say this to them? Are possessions wrong in themselves? Ought they not to take advantage of the technological age in which we live and have a better standard of living than their parents? A multiplicity of possessions is not a bad thing necessarily, but enslavement by them to the exclusion of higher things is. Down the ages there have been many people who have served Christ in their wealth, as also in their poverty. The important thing for Stephen and Jennifer, as for the rich young man and ourselves, is to get priorities right. Seek first the kingdom of heaven. Serve God. Love your neighbour. This can be done with or without many possessions, but there is a danger that we may become enslaved by our possessions and therefore fail.

SIXTH SUNDAY AFTER PENTECOST

Dead or alive?

> St. Luke 15.32 (NEB) *'How could we help celebrating this happy day? Your brother here was dead and has come back to life, was lost and is found.'*

INTRODUCTION

Where do your sympathies lie? With the younger or the elder brother? With the son who has behaved decently and remained at home, or with the scoundrel who has returned home after leading a spendthrift and dissolute life?

The younger brother

Life at home was a bore. All he could see ahead was years of repetitive boredom in the family situation. Working on the farm by day; little by way of pleasurable pursuits in his leisure time. He longed to get away from it all. His father might live for many years. What was the use of an inheritance when you're too old to enjoy it? He knew that with a bit of persuasion the old man would give him his share of the inheritance. The father was wise and let him go free, although he had misgivings about the son going away. How would he use his freedom in the city? This was a risk a loving father took. Jesus tells us of the riotous living of this young man: the wasting of his capital; high life with the permissive set; deserted by them when his money runs out and he can no longer pay his share; unemployed; menial employment. A need is felt—hunger! A resolve is made to return home and seek forgiveness. The prodigal son returns to a welcome beyond his wildest dreams and the reception is not what he expected.

The elder son

'There's a job to be done. We're fortunate to have a family business and parents who have made a comfortable home for us and given us such a start in life. Pity the kid didn't see this; but he's so unreliable and cannot see the advantages of staying here. Still, that's his decision. Good heavens! What's that? A party. Not heard a din like that since the evening before he went away; his eighteenth birthday party. He's back! How dare he show his face here after the way in which he's behaved. They've killed the fatted calf! I'm not going in. It's not fair. Here I've been a loving and faithful son and how have I been treated? What's that Dad said? "Your brother here was dead and has come back to life, was lost and is found." Wish he were dead!'

Application

Where do your sympathies lie? Doubtless with the elder son, who was so reliable and honest and well-intentioned in all he did. Our sympathies should be with the elder son, but for a different reason: he has not realized in his self-righteousness that he is a sinner.

What are the truths which Jesus presents in this parable? All are sinners—including you and me. All need to recognize this and come to a point of decision. The decision freely made must be to 'Turn to Christ' and seek forgiveness: 'Lord, I am not worthy.'

The father in the parable went running to meet the prodigal on his return. Our loving Father has gone all the way to meet our needs as penitents. God so loved us that he gave his son as the means of our redemption. The loving Father is waiting to receive and forgive.

SEVENTH SUNDAY AFTER PENTECOST

Forgiveness

> St. Matthew 18.35 (NEB) '. . . *each forgive your brother from your hearts.*'

INTRODUCTION

No one can read the gospels without an awareness of the

unique forgiving attitude of Jesus. We need only remind ourselves of the cry from the cross, 'Father, forgive them; they do not know what they are doing' (St. Luke 23.34 (NEB)). Or again, his response to the penitent thief, 'I tell you this: today you shall be with me in Paradise' (St. Luke 23.43); the forgiving Saviour. The disciples had noticed this wonderful ability of Jesus to forgive people as he dealt with many in need of forgiveness during his ministry. Anxious to follow Christ's example, Peter asks if there is a limit to forgiveness. There is no limit, says Jesus; there can be no limit for there is no limit to God's forgiveness. Similarly there should be no limit to forgiveness among the brotherhood of the Church.

Jesus then tells a parable to illustrate all that forgiveness involves. The whole point of the parable of the king and his debtor is that unless we are able to forgive others we shall not be aware of our own need of forgiveness; and impenitent we shall remain unforgiven. We are not to see God as the king in the story, for God has offered forgiveness without any conditions other than our acknowledgement that we have sinned and as penitents we ask for his forgiveness.

Forgiveness is costly

Forgiveness is costly both to the forgiver and the forgiven. The debtor who misused his position of authority and mis-appropriated the king's revenue had to swallow his pride and ask for forgiveness and be prepared for his appeal not to succeed. The ruler was in an impossible position as regards the recovery of the debt and his original intention was to impose a sentence which would act as a punishment; not to obtain any satisfaction of the debt. When the official appealed for his mercy, he abandoned this intention to punish and forgave the man his offence; this was costly.

Forgiveness the means of reconciliation

In forgiving the man the ruler was restoring the official to his former relationship. This was an act of reconciliation. Both would find it difficult to forget the cause of the offence; nevertheless reconciliation and restoration was effected. Consider a case where a husband is unfaithful to his marriage vows. It may be an isolated occasion when a passionate impulse, a favourable opportunity and circumstance cause him to commit adultery. He is so ashamed afterwards, and so loves his wife that he finds no alternative but to confess to her his infidelity. Both will find it difficult to forget this unfortunate incident. But loving each other forgiveness is sought and given. Reconciliation takes place and their relationship is restored.

Application

We cannot appreciate the extent of our indebtedness to God for the wonderful grace of his forgiveness unless we experience forgiveness in our human relationships. When we forgive others we are reminded that to forgive is frequently painful and always costly. This enables us to recollect the costliness of man's salvation and the pain which Christ endured on the cross. When we are forgiven by others we experience reconciliation and realize what it means to be restored into our true relationship to God through Christ. Forgiveness is an experience of the heart. The depth and sincerity of forgiveness are the criterion of its worth. 'Enable me to forgive others from my heart.' Christian action at its best is almost always a reaction to God's action. We are able to forgive others because he first forgave us. The cost of our forgiving is minimal compared with the cost of man's forgiveness on Calvary.

EIGHTH SUNDAY AFTER PENTECOST

Witness for the prosecution

St. John 15.27 (NEB) *'And you also are my witnesses. . . .'*

INTRODUCTION

We are called by Jesus to a decisive and dedicated discipleship.

He calls us, as he called his first followers, to witness in the world that Christianity works. Men and women in our technological age are still searching for a living faith and the question which they ask of the Church is, 'Does it work?' Demonstration that it works depends upon the way in which the dedicated disciple lives—Jesus said, 'I appointed you to go on and bear fruit, fruit that shall last' (St. John 15.16)—an effective witness of the eternal truth of the gospel.

What shall we witness?

The testimony of a witness in a court of law must express the truth as a particular person has witnessed it. The testimony must stand up to intensive cross-examination if it is to be of value. The Christian in the world is to be a witness for the prosecution, not for the defence of Christianity. We are to positively proclaim the truth that Christ is Lord. We shall be under heavy cross-examination all the time. What is unique about the Christian faith? How does it compare with other creeds—rival religious faiths and the compulsive creed of communism?

The hatred of the world which we encounter differs from that experienced by the apostolic church. The apostles proclaimed their faith in a situation where other faiths had a prior existence. Either a pagan faith (and the implications of Christian living ran contrary to the accepted tenets of the pagan faith), or the Jewish faith (a faith based upon a long-accepted belief that they were the chosen people and that YAHWEH was their God), which proved obstinate to the claims that Jesus Christ was the Son of the Living God. So Jesus warned his disciples that they would be hated by the world as he had been hated by the world.

How shall we witness?

The hatred of the world which we encounter differs from that experienced by the apostles. We live in a post-Christian Britain, where tradition, customs and culture still reflect Christian influences. Many people have a sneaking feeling that there may be some truth in Christianity after all. They don't want to write it off altogether; they label themselves 'agnostics'; or some even call themselves Christians, but add: 'I don't go to church'; a contradiction if ever there was one. Such doubters do not want Christianity to be proved true, it would demand too much from them in terms of love and service to accept Christ as Lord and Saviour. And so they hate us for reminding them that a decisive decision to discipleship is necessary. We are not in a persecution situation (though there are plenty of examples of martyrdom in the twentieth-century Church), instead they pound us with the question: 'Does it work?'

Application

We are called upon to witness that our faith does work, but we cannot do this in our own strength. We are witnesses, 'because you have been with me from the first' (St. John 15.27). The beginning for us was baptism, when we received the gift of the Holy Spirit. The indwelling Holy Spirit enables us to bear witness for the prosecution—'Christianity does work!' Others will assess the truth of our claim by the manner of our living as known followers of Jesus.

NINTH SUNDAY AFTER PENTECOST

Prophets in our time

> St. John 17.18 and 19 (JB)
> '*As you sent me into the world,*
> *I have sent them into the world,*
> *and for their sake I consecrate myself*
> *so that they too may be consecrated in truth.*'

INTRODUCTION

There is some urgency about this priestly prayer of Christ. His work must very soon be continued by a small band of followers. For them he prays, as also, 'for those also who through their words will believe in me' (St. John 17.20). We are among those for whom he prays.

Keep them true to your name

All Christians are to follow in the prophetic tradition of the Old Testament, to proclaim the truth about God and the facts and significance of Christ's life, passion and death, resurrection and ascension. Jesus prays that his followers may be true to God's name. As prophets we are to proclaim the ways of God to the wills of people from the heart. This is no easy task as people are wilful and the truths which are to be proclaimed will always bring violent opposition. It was certain that the apostles would suffer for Christ's sake and the kingdom. Their hearts would be broken. Prophecy involves suffering: the Old Testament prophets always suffered. Nevertheless disciples must remain true to their prophetic calling and Jesus prays that this may be so. He prays for all God's people today who are called into the same prophetic ministry: clergy and people. We seek to know the mind and will of God and to proclaim it in contemporary terms to people today. We encounter opposition and suffering. There can be no compromise with the world. Compromise is one of the devil's principal weapons. What stand are we making in the secular situation today? Where are our moral standards? Where shall social justice be found? Only in accord with God's will.

Protect them from the evil one

The gospel proclaims the victory of God. A proclamation so glorious and world-shaking is disastrous for the evil one. So he plans to destroy the effectiveness of the Church today. The devil is devious and subtle in all his ways and thus we fail to recognize his destructive activities. How does he seek to destroy? Contemporary mass-communication provides the evil one with a more powerful means of destruction. Under the pretence of Satire the Church is subjected to derisive forces: get people to laugh at the Church and they will be blind to the truth that this undermines her work and witness. In many other ways the evil one is active. Consider the scale upon which evil is present in the world today: man's inhumanity to man, terrorist regimes, and the ever-present threat of nuclear destruction. We are powerless on our own, so Christ prays 'protect them from the evil one'.

Consecrate them in truth

Powerless on our own; powerful in the strength of Christ. Thus Jesus prays and acts. 'For their sake I consecrate myself so that they too may be consecrated in truth' (St. John 17.19). Power and truth is in Christ crucified, risen and ascended. We do not proclaim this victory with sufficient emphasis. We need to proclaim that God's victory has been won; that we are on the winning side.

Application

We are sent into the world with the same divine command that sent the apostles out on their mission. Like them we are to know the will and purposes of God. Copying their example we are to proclaim the *entire* activity of God with its victorious certainty. We have been consecrated through the suffering servant; and if we are true to our prophetic calling we shall also suffer for the sake of Christ and his kingdom. The violence of the opposition may well indicate that we are fulfilling in our time our prophetic role. 'I wish that all the Lord's people were prophets' (Numbers 11.29).

TENTH SUNDAY AFTER PENTECOST

Servants of God

St. John 13.15 (NEB) '*I have set you an example. . . .*'

INTRODUCTION

Technological developments have facilitated the introduction of labour-saving devices into our homes: washing machines, dishwashers, Hoover cleaners and the like enable the housewife to pursue her domestic work with greater ease. This does not mean that she is not still a servant to the household, caring for husband and children with many attendant chores. No machine can substitute for the loving care of a mother for her baby: regular feeding, changing of nappies, careful bathing of the dependent child. The mother is in control; nevertheless she is the servant of her baby.

Economic and social changes have reduced employment in domestic service to a small number of men and women. No longer is there the hierarchy of basement and attic dwellers in the establishment of the large house: butler, housekeeper, chambermaid and so on. No longer is it considered desirable employment to be a servant. But Jesus said, 'I have set you an example.'

The occasion

'It was before the Passover festival' (St. John 13.1), that Jesus took water and a towel and washed his disciples' feet. The disciples were preparing to keep the feast, recalling that heroic occasion in their national history when by divine intervention their ancestors were delivered from the Egyptians. They would recollect that Moses, the leader on that occasion, was a Servant of God. Jesus taught by example and word what it means to be a Servant of God. 'I have set you an example.'

The servant of God

The washing of the disciples' feet was a prelude to Christ's supreme act of service as the suffering servant. His whole life had been one spent in the service of God and of his fellow-men. He was (as he said on this occasion) their Lord and Master— the Leader upon whom they depended, upon whom we can depend with certainty and hope. A curious mixture this: to lead and yet to serve. There is a particularly relevant word which defines the role both for Christ and his followers. We speak of the *ministry* of Jesus. From the earliest days of the apostolic church to the present time there has been a succession of men called by God to be his ministers, leading the people of God and yet in their service.

Application

At the present time we are increasingly aware that all Christians are called to be Servants of God, recognizing a wider ministry of the whole Church. Much is now said about being the Servant Church, the chosen people expending themselves in the service of the kingdom. God's servants in his world, where God is in control. How are we to be servants of God? The two illustrations used at the beginning of this sermon can give us some guidance.

The mother is the willing servant (almost slave) of her baby, although she knows that in time he will grow independent of her. We are to be willing servants in the Church's ministry in the world, even though our service may be abused, just used or even rejected. The second illustration was of the servants in the large household. Their employers were dependent upon them. Dependency meant that each and every servant fulfilled his or her specific tasks in the entire domestic structure of the household. God depends upon us; depends upon each member of the Church fulfilling his or her specific tasks using the special gifts which God has given to each one of us. Jesus said, 'I have set you an example'. Do we follow Christ's example?

ELEVENTH SUNDAY AFTER PENTECOST

Where are you going?

St. John 13.36 (NEB) '*Lord, where are you going?*'

INTRODUCTION

Where are you going? On a business trip or to take the family to see friends or maybe setting off on your annual holiday?

If you are going to a place for the first time, then you will wisely plan your route before commencing your journey. You may even obtain a detailed route plan from the AA or RAC to prevent your getting lost. On the journey you will also need to observe those general directions for all motorists—the signs of the Highway Code—otherwise your danger will be greater than merely getting lost.

We are not able to discover detailed directions in the New Testament to guide us in our own individual Christian life. There are, however, general directions given by Jesus enabling us to plan our lives in accord with God's will. General directions, when observed, keeping us in a God-ward direction.

Follow me

This is a personal call to each of us. A call which came to Peter and the other disciples. They immediately left their work. Many men and women throughout the centuries of the Christian Church have left lucrative employment and gone out as missionaries to all parts of the world. The disciples left their homes and followed Jesus. Following Jesus was all that seemed to matter to them, but their discipleship turned out to be quite different from what they imagined when first they answered the call, 'Follow me.' Our discipleship will take us into many unexpected places and situations.

You cannot follow me now

Peter must have been astonished to hear Jesus say these words. For years he had been with Jesus only to be told, 'you cannot follow me now.' We know (as Peter was soon to learn) that Jesus had to tread the road to Calvary alone. Peter was to discover (as we know only too well) that Jesus was to return to the Father at his Ascension. There were other reasons why Peter was prevented from following Jesus at that time. Jesus had work for Peter to do. Peter was not yet ready for that work. Indeed in terror for his own life he denied that he knew Jesus. Nevertheless Peter's leadership proved vital to the continuing work of the risen and ascended Christ.

One day you will follow me

Peter was promised that this would be so; in God's good time. This is a promise made by Jesus to all faithful people. 'I am going there on purpose to prepare a place for you' (St. John 14.2); 'Where I am you may be also' (St. John 14.4).

Application

From these general directions given by Jesus we are to find our way to God, in prayer and fellowship. The days of sacrificial response to the call, 'Follow me' are not yet past. There will be times when we shall pray to be released from a situation which seems intolerable. We may even pray to be delivered by death. But the answer may be: 'you cannot follow me now.' We must willingly embrace each situation for God's sake, knowing that one day we shall follow Jesus to a place prepared for us, where he has gone before.

TWELFTH SUNDAY AFTER PENTECOST

Ends and means

> St. John 17.20 (NEB) *'But it is not for these alone that I pray, but for those also who through their words put their faith in me; may they all be one. . . .'*

INTRODUCTION

Jesus at prayer. We can feel the intensity of his prayer to the Father in a prayer which began with intercession for his disciples to whom he was to entrust his work; then prayer for disciples of all generations.

Ends and means

'But it is not for these alone that I pray, but for those also who through their words put their faith in me.' A prayer for the

apostles in their vocation; an 'end' in themselves, called out of
the world, responding to that compulsive call of Christ, 'Follow me.' But they are called for service; to win others to discipleship of the Lord. They are a 'means' as well as an 'end'. We
must not forget that we, as disciples 'who put their faith in
Christ', are entrusted with the same task of winning others for
Christ. We are to Jesus 'ends' in ourselves and 'means' to other
ends.

Means to an end

The 'end' which must always be kept in view is the mission of
the Church that 'the world may believe that thou didst send me'
(v. 21). Why is this so important? Surely, as we recognize and
accept Jesus as the One sent by God, so we acknowledge and
share in the revealed purpose of God. A relevation made through
the Cross of Christ and through the action of the Spirit. A
revelation we make known to all mankind that they may believe and share in the Christian inheritance.

The shared inheritance

In most areas of life—school, industry, leisure activities and
hobbies—there are beginners and those with greater experience.
Those with greater experience are entrusted with greater responsibility and often called to leadership. Sometimes they
hang on to that responsibility and position longer than they
should. But we all know that in human institutions it usually
takes time to reach positions of responsibility and new-
comers must expect no immediate recognition. Not so in the
Church; if she is true to her divine founder. Jesus prayed—'may
they all be one'—the new converts whom the Apostles would
bring into the fellowship as well as the existing apostolic eleven.
'May they all be one: as thou, Father, art in me, and I in thee,
so also may they be in us' (v. 21). This is the unity of the Christian Church for which Christ prayed and prays. Archbishop
Temple (himself a leader in ecumenical endeavour) wrote:

> 'The way to the union of Christendom does not lie through committee-
> rooms, though there is a task of formulation to be done there. It lies

through personal union with the Lord so deep and real as to be comparable with His union with the Father'.*

Application

Although we must share in the ecumenical endeavour of our time there is a prior unity we must achieve as individual Christians and corporately here in this place. We seek a personal union with the Lord so deep and real as to be comparable with his Union with the Father. A union made possible by Christ—made available to us in the eucharist in a very special sacramental provision. Sharing in that deeper union with Christ we are to remember that although 'ends' in ourselves we are also 'means'. You and I have a responsibility to share in the mission of the Church to bring the whole world to believe in Christ as the Son of God.

THIRTEENTH SUNDAY AFTER PENTECOST

Mission to the world

St. John 16.8 (NEB) *'When he comes. . . .'*

INTRODUCTION

Scientific knowledge has increased our awareness of the universe; its vastness and complicated pattern. Technological developments, on the other hand, appear to have made the world a much smaller place as 'means of communication' have brought peoples and nations into a closer proximity and knowledge of each other. Scientific and technological advances have also created problems. What has not changed in character is 'the world' as theologically defined and understood; 'Human society seeking to direct its life without God.' It includes the agnostic as well as the atheist. Indeed it includes all men until

*William Temple, *op. cit.*, pp. 311 and 312.

in Christian commitment an individual responds to the power of the Holy Spirit; a power which Christ says will be evident in three directions.

Confute

In this activity the Spirit proves false any arguments against the claims of Jesus. The Spirit shows how sinfully wrong were the Jews to reject God's appointed messenger. He shows twentieth-century man how sinfully wrong he is to reject Jesus as the Son of God. The Paraclete shows where 'wrong and right and judgment lie' (v. 8).

Convict

In the power of the Spirit, on the Feast of Pentecost, Peter preached with such conviction that the assembled crowd when they heard what he had to say 'were cut to the heart' (Acts 2.37). He produced the precise effect of a conviction of sin. The Spirit convicts the world 'of wrong, by their refusal to believe in me' (v. 9). The sin is in the rejection of Jesus, particularly in refusing to accept the reality of his redemptive act.

Convince

The Spirit, says Our Lord, 'will convince them that right is on my side ... [and of] divine judgment' (vv. 10 and 11). To convince someone is to firmly persuade them. The Spirit firmly persuades us of the truth and effectiveness of Christ's passion as a victory of God. Christ's death was not a criminal's just punishment, nor the victory of the devil. The Spirit shows us that in Christ's going to the Father, who receives him, Jesus' cause is vindicated. He shows us that this was divine judgment on the devil and all his works: 'the Prince of this world stands condemned' (v. 11). Thus the Spirit brings each person to a moral decision: for or against Christ.

Application

Jesus tells us of the Spirit's judgment of the world. How does the Spirit work? The clue is to be found in the Acts of the

Apostles and the Epistles. The Spirit works through his Church; through you and me, men and women of the world who have responded to his power and indwelling with conviction. It remains the Church's mission 'to the world' to confute, convict and convince.

FOURTEENTH SUNDAY AFTER PENTECOST

Involvement

St. Luke 10.25 (NEB) '*Master, what must I do to inherit eternal life?*'

INTRODUCTION

Involvement! This is the criterion by which the Church is principally judged at the present time. Her critics consider that too much time is spent in discussing ecclesiastical structures and liturgical arrangements. The critics cannot, however, establish the extent of the Church's involvement in society solely by her official agencies and pronouncement of her leaders. Countless Christians give unstinted service in so many ways; their Christian commitment not known to those they assist. But the critics rightly remind us that Christians must be involved in the world. 'What must I do?' the lawyer asks. It is as though Jesus replied, 'You cannot hope to love God whom you have not seen, if you cannot attempt to love those whom you can serve.' The parable of the Good Samaritan is totally concerned with involvement.

Application

All of us need to be involved in activity for others, showing forth the love of God for mankind in our Christian commitment.

Taking the risk

The first step of involvement is taking the risk. The priest and the Levite were not prepared to take the risk of being involved. The Samaritan was prepared, even though he might have endangered his own life and property as he tended the injured man. Observe any incident today and see how many people are willing to be actively involved. Many stand by and watch. Taking the risk, without knowing in advance what it will be, is essential to Christian involvement.

Taking the care

The Samaritan took care of the injured man. He rendered first aid, and then he took him to the nearest place of rest and cared for him. Caring involves time and trouble. The Christian ought not to limit his caring for others simply to giving alms so that others may undertake the actual work. Giving Christian Aid is not enough. Rendering Christian Aid is part of our commitment to Christ. Are we prepared (for example) once a week to visit the same senior citizen and spend an hour with him or her, knowing that on each visit we shall be regaled with the same complaints. To undertake such care of older people is real involvement at personal cost.

Counting the cost

The injured traveller was alone until the Good Samaritan came along. This stranger did not count the cost: a cost in money and time as he brought the much-needed relief. There are many lonely people in our neighbourhood today just longing for someone to call. Such involvement can be costly in time and patience.

Love the stranger

This was certainly the case in the parable. The Samaritan had not seen the man before and it is more than likely that the injured man was not a Samaritan. This adds to the significance of the parable which Jesus told in answer to the questioning lawyer. Are we prepared to love the stranger and perform for him a neighbourly act? Remember these words: 'Lord, when was it that we saw you hungry and fed you, or thirsty and gave you drink, a stranger and took you home, or naked and clothed you? When did we see you ill or in prison, and come to visit you?' ... 'I tell you this: anything you did for one of my brothers here, however humble, you did for me' (St. Matthew 25.37–40).

FIFTEENTH SUNDAY AFTER PENTECOST

Disposition of a true disciple

St. Mark 10.15 (JB) *'Anyone who does not welcome the kingdom of God like a little child will never enter it.'*

INTRODUCTION

Anyone unconversant with the Christian faith hearing today's gospel for the first time, might well be excused in concluding that Christ was concerned on this occasion with divorce and children. It is true that the Church holds fast to the permanency of the marriage bond and in her ministry has ever provided for the care of children in their spiritual, educational and physical needs. But there is something more deeply relevant in Christ's teaching in today's gospel. Christ was concerned in his teaching with the establishment of the kingdom. Debate continues as to its inception, existence and eventual fulfilment. If, however, there was a new factor in God sending his Son and through him inaugurating the Kingdom of God, then all that Jesus says in relation to the kingdom *must* be considered against the claim that the kingdom is already established through him. Christ's comments on divorce and children must be considered in their relevance to the kingdom and our allegiance to the kingdom.

Application

Explained in terms of the Kingdom of God there are several

relevant considerations which we can explore under two main headings.

1. *Permanency of our relationship.* Jesus speaks of the permanency of the marriage bond. Divorce was permitted (to the husband only) under the Mosaic law, because of the weakness of man. Jesus is the fulfilment of the law and this changes the situation. The kingdom having been inaugurated, the permanency of our relationship to God becomes paramount (as well as the permanency of the marriage bond to any Christians who marry); a permanent relationship to God based upon trust and love. The basis of our permanent relationship is Christ 'the corner-stone'.

2. *Child-like acceptance.* Jesus had only just returned to an active continuance of his ministry among the people. He had been with his disciples giving them a clearer definition of their role in the Kingdom of God. His return to the public arena was heralded by the attempt of his enemies to trap him through an unwise proclamation concerning divorce. The crowds wanted him to bless their children and, anxious to protect their Master from the pressures upon him, his disciples tried to prevent parents from bringing their children to him. But Jesus was ready to receive them and took the opportunity to underline the qualities which all must possess if they are to welcome the kingdom of God. What are these childlike qualities which we must possess? At first we are inclined to think of the innocence and simplicity of children; but we are no longer innocent of the deep division between man and God nor unaware of our sinfulness. Our intellectual development and our wilfulness and pride make it difficult for us to accept a simple faith; we seek proof. It is here that the other qualities of childhood need to be recognized and adopted by Christians. We need to be unselfconscious about our Christian profession; not unduly worried by what others say. We need to be receptive to God's will. We must be content to be utterly dependent upon God, not anxious for the morrow or even today's needs. It is in such a spirit of dependency upon God that the kingdom must be received. This is the disposition of a true disciple.

SIXTEENTH SUNDAY AFTER PENTECOST

Entanglement

St. Matthew 22.21 (J B) *'Very well, give back to Caesar what belongs to Caesar—and to God what belongs to God.'*

INTRODUCTION

The presence of the imperial troops, and the residence of a Roman governor Pilate, were a constant reminder that the Jews lived under foreign rule. Government by the occupying imperial power created a division among the people. Supporters of the regime of the puppet king (Herod), whom the Emperor permitted a defined role in the local administration, exploited the advantages of this subsidiary relationship to the controlling power. Others—including the influential Pharisees—were opposed to the regime and anxious to overthrow Roman control.

Difficulties had been created by the appearance of a popular preacher and teacher, who appeared to the populace to speak and act with an authority the Herodians and Pharisees did not possess. It might have augured well for the Jewish community if this popular leader, reminiscent of the prophets of old, had led the zealots in the overthrow of the imperial power of Rome. It was increasingly evident that leadership of such a revolt could not be expected from Jesus. Instead from the point of view of those in authority in Jewry he was becoming a menace, if not a danger.

It would be to their advantage if they could get rid of him. Could they trap him and then bring some charge against him? How better to entangle him in political dispute than to raise the controversial question of paying tribute to Caesar? If he approves, then the Pharisees will immediately use this approval as a means to undermine the popularity of Jesus with the masses. If he opposes, the Herodians will take advantage of their position in the puppet regime to have him brought before Pilate as a danger to the occupying power of Rome.

'But Jesus was aware of their malice' and intrigue. He turned the tables upon them by the simple device of putting a question to them, asking whose 'head' was on the denarius handed to him. The coin belonged to Caesar, 'very well, give back to Caesar what belongs to him'; it is a debt owed. His reply took them by surprise and defeated their objective. But not before Jesus had used the incident to God's advantage: 'Give back . . . to God what belongs to God.' And to the chosen people the whole of life belongs to God.

Application

Inevitably Christians and the Church become entangled in political and social issues. On many political and social issues Christians are divided—we find Christians active in all the major political parties. This division may even be exploited by the enemies of the Church. But we are not to be afraid of entanglement provided that we observe the injunction of our Lord: 'Give back . . . to God what belongs to God.' This has a prior claim: our loyalty to Christ and giving to God the whole of our lives. This may bring us into conflict with the state, and twentieth-century experience has shown the consequences for Christians to be imprisonment, torture, even death. The age of martyrdom for Christ is not yet past. Are we prepared to become entangled for Christ to this extent?

SEVENTEENTH SUNDAY AFTER PENTECOST

How shall we build?

> St. Matthew 7.24 (NEB) *'What then of the man who hears these words of mine and acts upon them?'*

INTRODUCTION

If you or I were contemplating building a new house we

should not build upon sand, but we might suffer at the hands of a speculative builder unless we planned wisely.

When to build?

Ability to raise the necessary capital is a vital consideration and most people need to raise a mortgage and consider the sum of the monthly repayment which will have to be made. If these problems can be successfully negotiated there is no doubt that there is no time like the present to build. Prices have continued to rise, well-maintained and sited property is always in demand, and the possession of one's own house is a sound investment.

Where to build?

Great care must be taken in the choice of a site—its suitability to the needs of the owner–occupier being of first importance. There are other considerations to be borne in mind: for example, the likelihood of other building or road developments in the area, which might affect the amenities and the capital value.

What to build?

It is important that we think of our needs: future needs as well as the present needs; size of family and age of children here being most important. Having decided the kind of house we have in mind then we need to call in an architect to design the house in accordance with our general outline. This is important, as we shall be amazed at the number of factors we have failed to take into account and which need to be determined at the planning stage.

How to build?

We must build in accordance with the architect's plans; using the skills of the several craftsmen in the building industry; making certain that the house is based upon a sound foundation.

Application

Do we pay the same attention to the building of our lives purposefully as we would do to the planning and building of a new house? 'What then of the man who hears these words of mine and acts upon them?' We have heard the words of Jesus; how do we act upon them? The time to act upon them is NOW and Christ is the foundation. In the Old and New Testaments we can discover the plans of the divine architect of the universe —the design of God for mankind.

How do we build? We must take notice of the teaching of Christ and listen to God, but Jesus commends the man who ACTS. Yet in building our lives upon the firm foundation of Christ we are not building in isolation. There are the skills of other Christian people upon whom we can depend—the pastoral and spiritual skills of the parish priest, the teaching skills of competent laymen, the examples of countless Christian men and women in all ages. But above all there is the example of Christ our Saviour. We are able to build our lives upon a regular sacramental foundation. In this we shall be seen to be 'men of action' acting upon Christ's words; 'Do this in remembrance of me.' Acting in this way we are by no means speculative builders.

EIGHTEENTH SUNDAY AFTER PENTECOST

Claims and demands

> St. Matthew 5.21 and 22 (RSV) *'You have heard that it was said to the men of old. . . . But I say. . . .'*

INTRODUCTION

The short gospel passage we have just heard read makes some substantial claims and demands. Demands made by Jesus upon his followers; demands which were made in the light of the claims which Jesus made for himself.

The claims of Jesus

The claims which Jesus makes are to be found in the contrasting proclamations of verses 21 and 22. 'You have heard that it was said to the men of old.' What was said to the men of old in the enactment of the law and the proclamations of the prophets was usually prefaced by the words: 'Thus saith the Lord.' Such pronouncements were made at the express command of God. But note the contrast in verse 22. 'But I say. . . .' No 'Thus saith the Lord.' His hearers were astounded at his presumption which some regarded as blasphemous. Yet they could hardly avoid the conclusion that Jesus spoke with authority. The claims which Jesus made were based upon the truth that he was 'the only begotten of the Father, full of grace and truth' (St. John 1.14). In the light of this claim Jesus makes demands upon his followers.

The new law

The demand which Jesus makes amounts to a new law. The response which Jesus expects from his followers is a life of righteousness. Such a life demands an even more exacting law. Judgment applies to the condition of the inward motive, rather than the outward act. Jesus says, 'You are not to be angry with your brother', and we are to regard 'brother' as referring to anyone within the family of God. Jesus says, 'You are not to insult your brother': you are not to call him a fool, stupid or a block-head. This new law of love, appropriate to a life of righteousness, makes most exacting demands upon all Christians.

Be reconciled

No one can ever accuse Jesus of not putting duty and response to God as the first response of a man of God. A response expressed in worship; but here Jesus says, 'first be reconciled to your brother'. If he has offended you, go and forgive him. If you have offended him, go and ask for his forgiveness; a most difficult counsel for Christian perfection, for we have to begin by acknowledging that we are in the wrong. Be reconciled.

Application

The demands of righteous perfection which Jesus makes; are

they reasonable? The answer is 'Yes'. We are to watch our behaviour and see that is it consistent with our Christian profession. We must remember that perfection in the Christian life is only possible through the mercy of God. Utter dependence upon God's mercy is our only hope of fulfilling Christ's 'New Law' of Love. Thus we are constantly to pray for God's mercy —'Lord, have mercy'. Although it is improbable that any of us will commit murder, few (if any of us) can claim that we are never angry or never insult anyone. The inward motive reminds us that we are always in need of forgiveness and that we must always be ready to forgive. 'Forgive us our trespasses, as we forgive those who trespass against us.'

NINETEENTH SUNDAY AFTER PENTECOST

One Lord—three responses

> St. Luke 5.4 (NEB) *'When he had finished speaking, he said to Simon. . . .'*

INTRODUCTION

All Christians should find themselves making a three-fold response to Christ, as Peter did on the occasion recalled in today's gospel.

Obedience

Jesus said to him, 'Put out into deep water and let down your nets for a catch' (St. Luke 5.4). Christ's command came at an inopportune time. Peter was tired after the previous night's unprofitable labour. The command came in the hours of daylight when all knowledgeable fishermen knew from experience that there is not likely to be any catch. The instruction was given by a carpenter. Peter might well have refused to carry out this command—rational argument and expertise were on his side, and he was tired and ready for a well-earned rest. But there was something about Jesus that evoked a ready response from Peter.

Poverty

The unexpected catch took Peter and his partners by complete surprise—this they had not anticipated. Peter was overwhelmed by the evidence of this extraordinary experience. He was instantly aware of his own poverty and his utter dependence upon God for his well-being. Contrasting the munificence of God's goodness with the poverty of his own life—poverty of spirit, poverty of belief rather than lack of possessions—he was acutely aware of his own sinfulness and the need for forgiveness. This awareness and response to Jesus brought him into a deeper relationship.

Loyalty

Can we think of this in terms of 'faithfulness' making demands upon our lives? For Peter this meant giving up the security of his secular employment and following Jesus; it also meant that he left the comfort of his own home. This change of life Peter willingly embraced after his encounter with Jesus, the One Lord. Peter made three responses on this one occasion; which was the beginning of his discipleship.

Application

It is not uncommon for any Christian to be faced with a three-fold response to Christ. We might be experienced and settled in our own profession. Then suddenly we come up against a resistance, like coming up against a blank wall, and we are aware that God wants us to do something completely different. Our vocation is to be something new. The time may be inopportune so far as we are concerned—there are family commitments, work to be completed, unfulfilled engagements in our diary; but Jesus says, 'Put out into deep water.' The curious thing is that we do not drown. Instead we find that when we are obedient to the call of Christ we are amazed at the abundance of God's mercy. Then—like Peter—we see the poverty of our own lives and cry out, 'Lord, forgive.' The certainty and experience of God's forgiveness brings us into a deeper relationship with him. Often we long for this deeper relationship with God, but fail to recognize the poverty of our own response: the poverty of our prayer life, our limited efforts to love him. When we become aware of the poverty of our response and seek his forgiveness, in the abundance of his mercy and love, the relationship is deepened. Strengthened we find ourselves undertaking specific work for the kingdom; service which demands a loyal and faithful response from us.

TWENTIETH SUNDAY AFTER PENTECOST

The Lord's Prayer

St. John 17.1 (NEB) *'After these words Jesus looked up to heaven and said. . . .'*

INTRODUCTION

When the disciples asked Jesus to teach them 'How to pray', he gave them the familiar Lord's Prayer. Why did the disciples make this request? Because they had seen in Jesus a Man of Prayer and they wanted to be like him. Do we want to be men and women of prayer? Do we as Christians pray enough? Do we limit our prayers to the corporate prayers of the Church in her eucharistic worship, with perhaps an occasional outburst of private prayer when there is an emergency or 'when the spirit moves me'? We must all answer these and other searching questions on our prayer life for ourselves.

It may well be that like the disciples we do not know 'How to pray'. This Sunday morning we are provided with an opportunity of seeing Our Lord at prayer. A prayer which comprises the whole of the seventeenth chapter of St. John and is often referred to as 'The High-Priestly Prayer', or 'The Prayer of Consecration'. John Marsh, author of the Pelican Gospel Commentary of *St. John* has this to say:

> It is probably neither sheer coincidence nor the result of literary con-
> triving that the great prayer of ch. 17 echoes much of what has become
> known throughout Christendom as 'The Lord's Prayer'.*

In today's gospel the introductory eleven verses here provide an extension in depth of the opening petitions of the 'Our Father'. Prayer reflecting the relationship of Father and Son. Let us observe Our Lord at prayer and learn how to pray.

Application

Our Father. Jesus addresses God as Father. There is an intimacy of approach which reflects the relationship of Father and Son. An intimacy which can be observed in the prayers of children. A curate was in hospital having an operation; normally the prayers in church would be offered in such terms as, 'We pray for Father ——, Priest.' Not so the children of the top class of the church primary school at their weekly eucharist. They prayed—'We pray for Father —— who is having an operation on his knee'. They prayed conversationally, although they prayed to Jesus, 'Dear Lord. . . .' To whom do we pray? It should be in intimacy to the Father through the Son who enables us to pray in such a relationship to God the Father.

Hallowed be thy name. Jesus breaks with Jewish tradition. The name of God had been held with such awe and reverence that the name was never to be pronounced. Jesus has a different approach. He made known the name of God to his disciples (v. 6) and prays that they may be protected (as the new chosen people) by the power of God's name (v. 11). The Jews as the chosen people did not always hallow God's name; often they profaned it. The prophet proclaims the words of God when he tells them; 'It is not for your sake, you Israelites, that I am acting, but for the sake of my holy name, which you have pro-

---

* John Marsh, *St. John*. Pelican Gospel Commentaries, 1968, p. 553.

faned among the peoples where you have gone' (Ezekiel 36.22). God's holiness is revealed through his action. 'When they see that I reveal my holiness through you, the nations will know that I am the Lord, says the Lord God' (Ezekiel 36.23). Do we hallow God's name? Is his holiness revealed through us? We find the holiness of God revealed through Christ. Christ's prayer was lived out in his life. Is our prayer and living similarly integrated?

TWENTY-FIRST SUNDAY AFTER PENTECOST

God's ploughman

St. Luke 9.62 (RSV) *'No one who puts his hand to the plough and looks back is fit for the kingdom of God.'*

INTRODUCTION

At harvest-time we cheerfully sing,

> We plough the fields, and scatter
> The good seed on the land. . . .

yet few of us have any share in the production of our food. Only skilled men may plough. As we motor through the countryside at the right season of the year, we cannot but admire the contours of the newly-ploughed fields and reflect upon the skill of the ploughman. Mechanized agriculture has eased the labour of men on the land, but the tasks and skills are not less than in more primitive ploughing. There are four guiding principles which every ploughman needs to observe. These may also be applied to the life of every Christian.

Application

Consider these principles as they apply to your life, as I must do. Consider them as they apply to the corporate life of the Church.

Don't look back

We can well imagine the disaster which would immediately result from even a momentary looking-back by a ploughman. The course upon which he was set will not be followed. No longer will the furrow be straight. An even more disastrous consequence from the lack of concentration upon the task in hand will result in the ploughing being at an insufficient depth. Paul in his letters to the churches frequently alludes to the former state of the unbeliever and urges the Christian fellowship not to lapse into their former ways. 'Don't look back', he says. Our Lord is very firm to the man who first wanted to bury his father and the second man who wanted to say farewell to his family. 'No man who puts his hand to the plough and looks back is fit for the kingdom of God.'

Straight ahead

The aim of the skilful ploughman is to plough a straight furrow. To be Christ-like is our constant aim. 'Make straight the way of the Lord' (St. John 1.23). This is the way of the kingdom.

Hard work

Observing the ploughman at work we are aware of the intensity of effort. Work is to be accomplished within the limits of time imposed by the hours of daylight and favourable weather conditions. So must the Christian work hard and endure.

Forward in hope

The ploughman's thoughts are on the future. His work is a work of hope, looking forward to the next season's crop. Our Christian incentive should always be a looking forward in hope. Our hopes are many: that God's Will will be done; that his kingdom will come. Our hope is fixed on the reality and reliability of the kingdom of God. Our task is to share in its fulfilment and this requires of us that we should not look back, but aim straight at eternal truths in Christ; working without ceasing for the kingdom. We are God's ploughmen in this generation.

TWENTY-SECOND SUNDAY
AFTER PENTECOST

Universal religion

St. John 4.23 (NEB) *'But the time approaches, indeed it is already here, when those who are real worshippers will worship the Father in spirit and in truth.'*

INTRODUCTION

The universality of the Christian religion is clearly indicated in today's gospel, an episode in the continuing story of God's purposes in Christ. If we approach today's episode in the manner of a serial story, perhaps we can recover something of the excitement and anticipation which first we had for the bible stories. Imagine a continuing radio serial.

Yesterday we were listening to the dramatic presentation of an encounter at the Well of Jacob. Jesus was there. Thirsty after his journey, he takes the unusual action of asking a strange woman for a drink. The episode develops and we are able to identify the characters. We are already familiar with Jesus and his disciples, having met them many times in previous episodes. The woman of Samaria was a new character. But we were left in anticipation as the presentation came to an end. 'Sir, give me that water, and then I shall not be thirsty, nor have to come all this way to draw.' How will the story continue? Will Jesus put her right about the true nature and source of the living water?

And so we wait with anticipation for today's instalment. It begins with an unexpected twist to the story. 'Go home, call your husband and come back.' The living water is not to meet physical needs, but spiritual ones and it is soon apparent that the woman is much in need of spiritual help. Nor is the living water for selfish use; it is to be shared. Why not with one's married partner? All is not well, the woman is many times divorced and she is now living with a man to whom she is not married. She tries to wriggle out of this awkward situation

96

by raising a controversial issue between Jews and Samaritans: where is God to be worshipped? So runs the narrative, but this gospel episode has a deeper meaning—Christianity is *the* universal religion and the whole world must worship God in spirit and in truth.

Application

Water symbolizes the universality of our faith, a recurrent theme in the early chapters of the fourth gospel. The water offered to the woman of Samaria is the same living water offered to us, a continuous supply ever welling up within the individual who receives Christ, and satisfying all our desires.

The universality of the Christian faith is emphasized in the nature of true worship—not in Jerusalem nor on Mount Gerazin. True worship is possible through Christ's redeeming work which demands a universal response. 'Real worshippers will worship the Father in spirit and in truth.' We see God identified in Christ—God is Spirit—his essential being an infinite spiritual power in action. And we in spirit and truth respond as creatures worshipping our creator in eucharistic worship.

TWENTY-THIRD SUNDAY AFTER PENTECOST

The generosity of God

St. Matthew 20.15 (J B) '*Why be envious because I am generous?*'

INTRODUCTION

How magnificently Our Lord could tell a story. The parable of the labourers in the vineyard is no exception. His opening description of the owner making an agreement with the labourers at the beginning of the day immediately gives authenticity to the story. His listeners would be aware of this method of employing casual labour in the vintage season. They would not quarrel with the employment of the additional labourers for the last hour of the working day; the gathering of the crop was essential. But their surprise might have surpassed that of the labourers in the parable when Jesus told how the employer had paid all the workers the same day's pay. This was the surprise element in the story and gives it relevance. Equal pay for unequal effort; contrary to all sound economic policy.

There is debate among scholars concerning the placing of this parable: as a parable of the kingdom (which St. Matthew's account suggests), or Christ's answer to his critics that he dined with publicans and sinners. However, the main point of the parable is the generosity of God.

Agreement

The employer went out to the men in the market place: no question of bargaining about the rates of pay. An offer is made to them which they can accept or reject. God made a covenant with Abraham. The Jews were a covenanted people, free to accept or reject God's promise. The Jews contemporary to our Lord could benefit as much from the covenant as their ancestors before them, if they readily accepted the generosity of God. A new covenant was then made by God in the redemptive passion and death of Christ. Christians of this generation share equally with those of other ages in the agreement which God has made for the benefit of mankind.

Fair shares

The complaint made by the employees was solely on the grounds of fair returns for a fair day's work. There was no question that the agreement had not been fulfilled. They objected to the other labourers receiving the same pay and thought that they were entitled to superior treatment. The Church today sometimes reflects this same attitude. Members of a congregation with longer association in a parish church expect superior treatment and are disgruntled when new people take on an active role. Sometimes we act in a very un-Christian manner over comparative trivialities. Compare this with the generosity of God.

Generosity of God

The point which Jesus is making is the compassionate generous nature of God. The employer in the story knew the difficulties of making ends meet. Casual labouring at harvest time was essential to many families to supplement a subsistence economy. The employer did not enquire too closely from those still idle in the late afternoon as to why they were unemployed. He did not ask if they had tried elsewhere or were they merely lazy. He employed them and then out of his compassion for them he paid them handsomely, not as a reward for their labour, but having regard for their needs. God does not reward us according to our labour in the kingdom. We cannot earn our way to heaven. We have to place ourselves in a position of utter dependence upon the generosity of God's mercy, of which we possess ample evidence.

NINTH SUNDAY BEFORE CHRISTMAS

Rejected or accepted?

> St. John 1.11 and 12 (RSV) *'And his own people received him not. But to all who received him, who believed in his name, he gave power to become children of God.'*

INTRODUCTION

'Once upon a time. . . .' Those four magical words take us back to our childhood days, when we first heard or read Cinderella and other fairy tales. The characters and situations in these tales varied; yet each was based upon a simple formula—the conflict between good and evil, ending with the victory of good over evil.

St. John might well have written 'once upon a time' instead of 'In the beginning', or 'when all things began' as the *New English Bible* translates it. But the prologue to the fourth gospel is no fairy tale. It proclaims that God is active from the beginning and that his activity can be discerned in the Christ whom John proclaims. As I have my *New English Bible* open, I read on one page (at the end of St. Luke's gospel)—*The Final Conflict*; and on the next page (at the beginning of St. John's) —*The Coming of Christ*. The shadow of the cross extends over the babe in the crib. Here indeed is *the* conflict with an unexpected ending. Evil had apparently triumphed finally in the cruel death on Calvary, but God turned this into the victory of Christ. 'And his own people received him not. But to all who received him, who believed in his name, he gave power to become the children of God.'

Rejected

At the beginning there was no room for him in the inn. He was not recognized as the promised and long-awaited Messiah. The populace deserted him when he did not lead them in revolt against the political domination of Rome. Judas betrayed him. Peter denied him. His disciples fled after his arrest. Thomas doubted that he had risen.

Accepted

There is another side to the story. The inn-keeper did offer some accommodation and shepherds did rejoice at his birth. His contemporaries did believe that he did all things well. There were disciples who gave up all and followed him. Peter wept. John and Mary remained at the foot of the cross. Thomas did cry, 'My Lord and my God' (St. John 20.28).

Application

He gives us power to become children of God. A power so necessary in the world today when the conflict between good and evil is as real as ever. The prior condition is that we believe in his name. Believe in Jesus as Christ our Lord. There are many who accept the Jesus of Nazareth and each year celebrate the anniversary of his birth; but how many will exclaim with Thomas, 'My Lord and my God.' Behind the philosophical argument of John's prologue is the certainty that God came unto his own. Do you reject or accept him as human and divine?

EIGHTH SUNDAY BEFORE CHRISTMAS

Judgment

> St. John 3.18 (RSV) *'He who believes in him is not condemned; he who does not believe is condemned already, because he has not believed in the name of the only Son of God.'*

INTRODUCTION

Do you read detective stories? If so, I wonder what kind of reader you are? Do you carefully search for clues enabling you to identify the suspect? Or do you first turn to the end of the story to see how the author brings it to a conclusion? This latter sort of approach would spoil a detective story for me, though I can see that it may help in looking for the clues which the author has planted. On the other hand, it may hinder our identification of clues.

Our knowledge of the gospel-ending may hinder or aid us in looking for clues which the gospel writers provide; clues that are relevant to our understanding of Christ's whole mission, ministry and redemptive purpose. There is such a clue (which we might well miss) in St. John 3.18: that all who come into contact with our Lord come also into judgment. Possessing this clue and knowing the end of the gospel narratives that Christ died and rose again, what discoveries can we make in the gospels if we approach them with the same freshness as when we read a detective story?

(i) *The group judgment*

All the four gospels reveal the same evidence that very early on in his ministry we can discover groups whose final attitudes towards Jesus are implicit from the outset. On the one hand there are the disciples, whose belief in Jesus is recorded when he performed the first miracle in Cana of Galilee: 'This, the first of his signs, Jesus did at Cana of Galilee, and manifested his glory; and his disciples believed in him' (St. John 2.11). On the other hand there are the scribes, pharisees and priests. We are soon aware of their growing opposition to Jesus and the final conflict is not unexpected if we have carefully followed the narrative.

(ii) *The individual judgment*

In the case of individuals who come into contact with Jesus, the judgment is apt to appear as a process. On the one hand we read of an increasing enlightenment, as in the case of the woman of Samaria at the well, which concludes with her witness: 'Come, see a man who told me all that I ever did. Can this be the Christ?' (St. John 4.29). On the other hand we find an individual who, although not committing himself to a definite unbelief—a person we would call an agnostic, it is evident that he responds imperfectly to our Lord. Such a man was Nicodemus, the intellectual, to whom Jesus said, 'If I have told you earthly things and you do not believe, how can you believe if I tell you heavenly things?' (St. John 3.12).

Application

The question which we must answer is that of the Samaritan woman: 'Can this be the Christ?' We have not met our Lord face to face. We have, however, come into contact with him in the community of Christ and in our reading of the New Testament. And all who come into contact with our Lord— remember Saul on the road to Damascus—come also into judgment. 'Can this be the Christ?'

SEVENTH SUNDAY BEFORE CHRISTMAS

Knowing God

St. John 8.54 (NEB). 'You say, "He is our God", though you do not know him.'

INTRODUCTION

When two young people have fallen in love, they should get to know all about each other as a sound basis for married life. Each other's likes and dislikes, interests and ambitions, family background. You can, however, get to know a lot about a person without ever knowing them. To really know a person you have to live together as intimately as Christian marriage presupposes: for mutual society, help and comfort . . . both in prosperity and adversity.

We now have to consider the truth that God is man's concern. Jesus says that we are to know God—his is our mutual society . . . both in prosperity and adversity

The Jews, our Lord said, did not know God. They were like our young lovers at the beginning of their relationship knowing only about each other. The Jews thought they knew all about God; they claimed Yahweh as their God and claimed to be his chosen people. They knew that they were in a covenant relationship with God as the descendants of Abraham. But they did not have that intimate relationship with God that Abraham had, and the prophets, and which Jesus himself had experienced. They had not got beyond the preliminary stage of knowing about God; they had not explored the full love relationship that is possible and desirable between God and man. Have we got beyond knowing about God and really knowing him like Jesus did?

Application

We are to know all about God and to know that he cares—that man *is* God's concern. This knowledge is available to us in scripture and brought to our understanding by the action of the Holy Spirit. But we must not forget that it is possible to get to know all about him and yet not know God. 'You say', said Jesus, '"He is our God", though you do not know him.' But of himself he said, 'But in truth I know him and obey him.' We can know God in the same way. We begin by accepting the truth that we are children of the same heavenly Father, that there is a father/child relationship to be explored. We have the fuller revelation through Christ of the nature of God. From our study of the relationship of Jesus with God we shall find that there are two particular conditions which universally apply. Firstly, that an intimate relationship with God is to be sought and developed in prayer, observing the intensity of Jesus' prayer, even on the Cross—'My God, my God, why hast thou forsaken me?'; 'Into thy hands I commit my spirit.' Secondly, thus knowing God we are to obey him.

SIXTH SUNDAY BEFORE CHRISTMAS

Food for life

St. John 6.34 (RSV) *'They said to him, "Lord, give us this bread always".'*

INTRODUCTION

The crowd had followed Jesus eager to hear his words. They had seen many healed, they marvelled at the signs which he had performed before their very eyes. They had benefited from his action in feeding them with a plentiful meal from the scanty resources of five barley loaves and two fish, the picnic lunch of one small boy. Enthusiastically they had sought to capture him so that they might proclaim him as their leader, as their king. But Jesus had escaped. And now they had caught up with him again on the other shore at Capernaum. That is the background to today's gospel.

Again the crowd had come to Jesus in their hunger. They had set aside all caution which should have taught them to go to their own homes. They come in hunger, because he had satisfied their physical needs, and now Jesus tells them not to labour for the food which perishes, like the manna in the wilderness. And yet, the manna which their ancestors had eaten in the wilderness to satisfy their physical hunger had come from God to satisfy a temporary need. Now they are told by Jesus that 'the bread of God is that which comes down from heaven, and gives life to the world'.

Life for the world. This is a promise highly to be prized and possessed. 'Lord, give us this bread always.' If this is true we shall never go hungry; we shall not be dependent upon suitable seasons and satisfying harvests. But the bread of life to which Jesus referred was himself—'I am the bread of life'. He knew that their needs were more than physical needs. He knows that our needs are more than physical needs. There exists a universal spiritual hunger, if only we would recognize this. It is this spiritual need which Christ satisfies. 'He who comes to me shall not hunger, and he who believes in me shall never thirst.'

Application

Knowing as we do that Jesus is the Bread of Life we should ever cry out, 'Lord, give us this food always'; which he does in each and every eucharist. But there are two conditions. Firstly, that we believe in him; for in so doing we are doing the work of God. Secondly, we must come to him. In eucharistic terms this means believing that this spiritual food—this bread and this wine—is the sustaining Body and Blood of Christ to those who receive by faith. The body broken; the blood outpoured. The life-giving effects of Calvary. This is the food which gives life to the world.

FIFTH SUNDAY BEFORE CHRISTMAS

On the alert

St. Matthew 24.44 (NEB) *'Hold yourselves ready. . . .'*

INTRODUCTION

Observe a goal-keeper in action.

Sometimes he is a lone figure pacing along his goal-line. All the play is at the other end of the field and apparently he has nothing to do, except pace up and down to keep himself warm in the bitter wintry weather. However, this is not true. He must always be on the alert—defence can quickly turn to attack on the soccer field.

Sometimes the situation is in reverse. All the play seems to be concentrated in the danger zone of his own goal area. He must then be ever on the alert, his eyes carefully directed towards the area of play, his legs, feet and hands ready to prevent the opposing team from scoring; knowing that he is the last line of defence; only the spectators are behind him. Goal-keepers must live dangerously, pouncing on the ball.

Occasionally, when one of his own team has committed an infringement within the penalty area, he alone has to anticipate the angle, direction and height of the ball as the penalty kick is taken. This requires agility of eye, mind and body to prevent a penalty goal being scored. He must be on the alert.

Application

The gospel for today tells of the need for the Christian to be ever on the alert. Although he is never really on his own the Christian may sometimes think that he is. Indeed the goal-keeper is not really on his own; his supporters are willing him to succeed. God wills us to succeed and we have the help of the Holy Spirit and the support of our fellow Christians. Nevertheless we can find ourselves in a position not dissimilar to the goal-keeper. It may seem that our spiritual life is running very smoothly; the difficulties and dangers of the evil one are far removed from our present experience; nothing to trouble our consciences or give us undue concern. It is then that we need to be on the alert. We may have been lulled into a sense of false spiritual security.

There are other times when we are assailed on all sides by evil thoughts and actions and, except for the grace of God, we might easily succumb to 'the superhuman forces of evil in the heavens' (Ephesians 6.12). At once we need to 'take up God's armour' (Ephesians 6.13) including 'the great shield of faith, with which . . . to quench all the flaming arrows of the evil one.' (Ephesians 6.16).

There are yet other times when our own individual witness may be of absolute importance. It may be that what we have to say to a friend who has suffered the bereavement of a loved one will be the means whereby he retains his Christian faith or perhaps finds it. Again it may be loving action which makes another person mindful of the love of God.

In every situation, like the goal-keeper, we need to be on the alert for our 'enemy the devil, like a roaring lion, prowls round looking for someone to devour' (1 Peter 5.8).